Foundations of Modern Sociology Series

Alex Inkeles, *Editor*

Social Change, *Wilbert E. Moore*
The Sociology of Economic Life, *Neil J. Smelser*
Modern Organizations, *Amitai Etzioni*
The Family, *William J. Goode*
What Is Sociology? An Introduction to the Discipline and Profession, *Alex Inkeles*
Social Stratification: The Forms and Functions of Inequality, *Melvin M. Tumin*
Community Social Structure, *Peter H. Rossi*
Theory and Method in the Social Sciences, *Paul F. Lazarsfeld*
The Sociology of Groups, *Theodore M. Mills*
Political Society, *William Kornhauser*
Societies: Evolutionary and Comparative Perspectives, *Talcott Parsons*
Deviance and Control, *Albert K. Cohen*

Foundations of Modern Sociology Series

what is sociology?

AN INTRODUCTION TO THE DISCIPLINE AND PROFESSION

Alex Inkeles, *Harvard University*

Prentice-Hall, Inc., *Englewood Cliffs, New Jersey*

Current printing (last digit):
15 14 13 12 11 10 9 8 7

Prentice-Hall Foundations of Modern Sociology Series
Alex Inkeles, *Editor*

Library of Congress Catalog No.: 64–13092.
Designed by Harry Rinehart

PRENTICE-HALL INTERNATIONAL, INC., *London*
PRENTICE-HALL OF AUSTRALIA, PTY., LTD., *Sydney*
PRENTICE-HALL OF CANADA, LTD., *Toronto*
PRENTICE-HALL OF INDIA PRIVATE LIMITED, *New Delhi*
PRENTICE-HALL OF JAPAN, INC., *Tokyo*

C-95241 (p), C-95242 (c)

acknowledgments

I wish to thank Nancy Boyden and Sharlee Segal for help in various forms, including typing, which facilitated my work on this book; Patricia Pajonas for dedicated and effective research and editorial assistance; Joseph Berliner, Daniel Levinson, Howard Schuman, and Edward Tiryakian for their critical reading of various chapters; and Alfred Goodyear and Wilbur Mangas of Prentice-Hall, who resisted every temptation to press for the manuscript before we were satisfied that it met standards appropriate to this series.

Alex Inkeles

***To Robert S. Lynd,** research pioneer,*

ardent teacher, searching critic

contents

the subject matter of sociology

one

Any attempt to set limits to a field of intellectual endeavor is inherently futile. Whatever boundaries we set will inevitably omit men whose work should be included. Yet when we stretch the boundaries to bring these men and these works within the field, we inevitably incorporate some we otherwise would have excluded. And what seems to us today firmly entrenched as part of our little community, may yesterday have been an alien enclave and tomorrow may have set itself outside our walls as an independent discipline trying to define its own boundaries.

Yet no student can rightfully be expected to enter on a field of study which is totally undefined and unbounded. If he must be responsible for everything, he will master nothing. Indeed he will flee in panic, and properly so. To define the limits of a field of inquiry may prove, in the long run, to have been only a gesture, but for a start some delimitation, however tentative, is indispensable. The danger is really not too great if we keep in mind that any boundaries we establish are an aid to understanding. They should serve as a loose cloak to delimit form, and not as a rigid suit of armor which is endlessly constraining no matter how useful for fighting off those from other disciplines making claims to the same territory.

Three Paths to a Definition

Three main paths are available for delineating the subject matter of sociology.

1. The historical, whereby we seek through study of the classic sociological writing to find the central traditional concerns and interests of sociology as an intellectual discipline. In brief, we ask: "What did the founding fathers say?"

2. The empirical, whereby we study current sociological work to discover those subjects to which the discipline gives most attention. In other words, we ask: "What are contemporary sociologists doing?"

3. The analytical, whereby we arbitrarily divide and delimit some larger subject matter and allocate it among different disciplines. We ask, in effect: "What does reason suggest?"

The historical approach has piety to commend it. It offers us the opportunity to benefit from the wisdom of the past. It enables us to understand issues which can be grasped only if we comprehend their background. Of course, people may read the same history quite differently. In addition, the historical method runs the risk of making our thinking rigid, since tradition may be poorly suited to deal with emerging problems of the present and the future.

The empirical method is least ambiguous; it mainly requires some form of counting. Of course, what contemporary sociologists emphasize in their work may be simply a passing fancy, having little connection with the important work of the past or little promise for the future. In the opinion of Professor Pitirim Sorokin, current sociological preoccupations are nothing but "fads or foibles," [1] and, in the view of C. Wright Mills, they indicate a decline of "the sociological imagination." [2]

The analytical approach is the least troublesome. A few lines of definition, a few more paragraphs of explanation, and we have it. This is a time-honored path followed continuously since it was first marked out by Auguste Comte, the father of sociology. But decrees dividing the realms of human learning have none of the force of law. Scholars and scientists go where their interests lead them; they study what they like when they wish; they are natural poachers with little regard for property rights and "no trespassing" signs. The arbitrary definition of fields of study, while often aesthetically satisfying, is, therefore, generally a poor guide to what is really happening. It presents a neat master plan, but for lack of effective zoning laws the factual structure of research often bears little resemblance to it.

There is no need for us to prejudge the issue. Each perspective may offer us something of value in understanding sociology. I have avoided imposing a "pre-packaged" definition of its subject matter, choosing instead to allow a conception to emerge from a diverse set of relevant materials. Since the method is inductive, it requires a bit of patience. Answers will not always be forthcoming straightway. Yet I trust that those which emerge more gradually will also fade away less rapidly. By this method of presentation, furthermore, I hope not only to delineate the subject matter of the field but, in the course of doing so, to communicate something of sociology's history and an impression of contemporary issues. Both are themes to which we will often return.

[1] Pitirim A. Sorokin, *Fads and Foibles in Modern Sociology and Related Sciences* (Chicago: Regnery, 1956).

[2] C. Wright Mills, *The Sociological Imagination* (New York: Oxford University Press, 1959).

It would not be entirely honest to say: "I let the facts speak for themselves." Facts may *speak* for themselves, but they cannot *select* themselves. I have, however, tried conscientiously to select the facts without prejudice, allowing a wide variety of points of view to be represented. Needless to say, included prominently among these points of view is my own. My objective is to develop a broad and inclusive conception of sociology. This requires searching for unifying themes and common bases of agreement. But I have made no effort to disguise the great diversity of opinion which exists, nor to deny the frequently deep disagreement which often divides the sociological community.

What the Founding Fathers Said

Professor Sorokin's standard work on *Contemporary Sociological Theories*[3] cites well over 1,000 men whose work is important enough to mention in a review of the development of modern sociology. The standard "history and interpretation" of the evolution of *Social Thought from Lore to Science*[4] by Howard Becker and Harry Elmer Barnes fills two volumes of 1,178 long pages, apart from notes and appendices. In the face of this massive array, who is to say which men define the sociological tradition?

There are four men, however, whom everyone in sociology, regardless of his special emphasis, bias, or bent, will probably accept as the central figures in the development of modern sociology. They are: Auguste Comte, Herbert Spencer, Émile Durkheim, and Max Weber. Together, they span the whole of the nineteenth and early twentieth century, during which modern sociology was formed. They represent the main national centers—France, England, and Germany—in which sociology first flourished and in which the modern tradition began. Each exerted a profound personal influence on the conception of sociology as an intellectual discipline. It seems particularly relevant, therefore, to explore their opinions about the proper subject matter of sociology.

Auguste Comte (1798–1857), who gave sociology its name, devoted more energy to expressing hopes for and to staking out the claims of sociology than to defining its subject matter. He felt that social science in his time stood in the same relation to its future as once astrology stood in regard to the science of astronomy and as alchemy stood in relation to chemistry. Only in the distant future, he argued, would the sub-division of the field become practicable and desirable, and for his time he felt it "impossible . . . to anticipate what the principle of distribution may be."[5] We cannot get from him, therefore, any list of topics or sub-fields of sociological interest.

Although Comte was reluctant to specify in detail the sub-fields of sociology, he did propose and consistently treat sociology as divided into two main parts, the social statics and social dynamics. These two concepts represent a basic division in the subject matter of sociology which in many different forms and guises appears throughout the history of the field and persists today. In the first case the major institutions or institutional complexes of society—such as economy, family, or polity—are taken to be the major units for sociological analysis, and sociology is conceived of as the

[3] Pitirim A. Sorokin, *Contemporary Sociological Theories* (New York: Harper, 1928).

[4] Howard Becker and Harry E. Barnes, *Social Thought from Lore to Science*, 2nd ed. (Washington, D.C.: Harren Press, 1952).

[5] Auguste Comte (H. Martineau, trans.), *The Positive Philosophy of Auguste Comte* (New York: Blanchard, 1855), p. 442.

study of interrelations between such institutions. In the words of Comte: "The Statical study of sociology consists in the investigation of the laws of action and reaction of the different parts of the social system." [6] The parts of a society, he argued, cannot be understood separately, "as if they had an independent existence." Instead, they must be seen "as in mutual relation . . . forming a whole which compels us to treat them in combination." [7] He referred to this principle of "universal social interconnection" as the "master-thought" of his whole approach.[8]

The second major division of sociology which Comte proposed he called social dynamics. If statics was to be the study of how the *parts* of societies interrelate, dynamics was to focus on whole societies as the unit of analysis and to show how they developed and changed through time. "We must remember," he said, "that the laws of social dynamics are most recognisable when they relate to the largest societies." [9] Comte rather believed that he already had the problem solved. He was convinced that all societies moved through certain fixed stages of development, and that they *progressed* toward ever increasing perfection.[10] This view will find few supporters today. Fewer still would acknowledge that the stages identified by Comte are those through which all societies in fact have passed or will pass. What is important for us to remember, however, is that Comte felt the comparative study of societies as wholes was a major subject for sociological analysis.

Herbert Spencer's (1820–1903) three-volume *Principles of Sociology*, published in 1877, was the first full-scale systematic study explicitly devoted to an exposition of sociological analysis. He was much more precise than Comte in specifying the topics or special fields for which he felt sociology must take responsibility. Thus, in the first volume of the *Principles* he urged that:

> The Science of Sociology has to give an account of [how] successive generations of units are produced, reared and fitted for co-operation. The development of the *family* thus stands first in order. . . . Sociology has next to describe and explain the rise and development of that *political organization* which in several ways regulates affairs—which combines the actions of individuals . . . and which restrains them in certain of the dealings with one another. . . . There has to be similarly described the evolution of *ecclesiastical structures* and functions. . . . The *system of restraints* whereby the minor actions of citizens are regulated, has also to be dealt with. . . . The stages through which the *industrial part* passes . . . have to be studied . . . [as well as] the growth of those regulative structures which the industrial part develops within itself. . . .[11]

The subject matter of sociology as Spencer defined it contains quite familiar elements. Here and there we must translate a term. For example, when he speaks of the "system of restraints" he is obviously referring to the subject which in modern sociology is called "social control." Otherwise we have no difficulty in relating the subject matter of sociology delineated by contemporary sociologists to the outline given by Spencer. In the order given

[6] *Ibid.*, p. 457.
[7] *Ibid.*, p. 458.
[8] *Ibid.*, p. 461.
[9] *Ibid.*, p. 466.
[10] We return to a fuller discussion of these evolutionary theories of social development in Chap. 3.
[11] Herbert Spencer, *The Principles of Sociology*, 3rd ed. Vol. I (New York: D. Appleton and Company, 1910), pp. 437–440.

in the quotation, the fields of sociology according to Spencer are: the family, politics, religion, social control, and industry or work. In addition, Spencer explicitly mentioned the sociological study of associations, communities, the division of labor, social differentiation or stratification, the sociology of knowledge and of science, and the study of art and aesthetics. An unbiased examination of the table of contents of Spencer's *Principles* in the light of contemporary work described in our next section suggests that the range of subjects with which sociology deals has been remarkably stable for a long period of time.

Spencer would by no means have agreed, however, that sociology was limited to a list of institutions like the family or to processes such as social control. He also stressed the obligation of sociology to deal with the interrelations between the different elements of society, to give an account of how the parts influence the whole and are in turn reacted upon, and in the process may transform or be transformed. As examples of such "reciprocal influences" he called attention to the effects of sexual norms on family life, and the relations between political institutions and other forms of regulating behavior such as religion and ceremonial activity. He also advised parallel study of the organization of the priesthood and other hierarchies to reveal "how changes of structure in it are connected with changes of structure in them." [12]

Spencer added yet another responsibility for sociology—namely, to accept the whole society as its unit for analysis. He maintained that the parts of society, although discrete units, were not arranged haphazardly. The parts bore some "constant relation" and this fact made of society as such a meaningful "entity," a fit subject for scientific inquiry. On these grounds he held that sociology must compare "societies of different kinds and societies in different stages." [13] To grasp the principles of sociology, he maintained, "we have to deal with facts of structure and function displayed by societies in general, dissociated, so far as may be, from special facts due to special circumstances." [14] Thus, the main division of sociological emphasis suggested by Comte is clearly evident in Spencer's thinking as well.

Émile Durkheim (1858–1917) did not set forth his conception of the proper subject matter of sociology in as full detail as did Spencer. We can, however, easily reconstruct his position from remarks he made in his *Rules of Sociological Method* and his various other writings.[15]

Durkheim frequently referred to what he called the "special fields" of sociology, and he clearly favored their widespread development. Sociology could not become science, he said, "until it renounced its initial and overall claim upon the totality of social reality [and distinguished] ever more among parts, elements, and different aspects which could serve as subject matters for specific problems." In reviewing his own work and that of his associates in France, he affirmed their joint "ambition to initiate for sociology what Comte called the era of specialization." [16] Durkheim clearly approved the idea that sociology should concern itself with a wide range of institutions and social processes. He said for example: "There are, in reality, as many

[12] *Ibid.*, p. 439.
[13] *Ibid.*, p. 442.
[14] *Ibid.*, p. 37.
[15] A number of these have been gathered in Kurt H. Wolff (ed.), *Émile Durkheim, 1858–1917: A Collection of Essays, with Translations and a Bibliography* (Columbus: Ohio State University Press, 1960), 463 pp.
[16] Durkheim, "Sociology," in Wolff (ed.), *Émile Durkheim*, p. 380.

branches of sociology, as many particular social sciences, as there are varieties of social facts." [17]

Durkheim made his position unmistakably clear in the outline he established for the early volumes of the first sociological journal, *L'Année Sociologique*. He divided the journal into seven sections, with numerous subsections under each major heading. In a typical issue the major sections were: General Sociology—including a sub-section on personality in the individual and the collectivity; Sociology of Religion; Sociology of Law and Morals, including sub-sections on political organization, social organization, and marriage and the family; the Sociology of Crime; Economic Sociology, including sub-sections on the measurement of value and on occupational groups; Demography, including a sub-section on urban and rural communities; and one on the Sociology of Aesthetics. This outline, dating from 1896, could easily be used for a contemporary general review of sociology.

Although taking a broad view of the institutions and social processes which sociologists might study, Durkheim, like Comte and Spencer, also emphasized the importance of analyzing the relationships among institutions and between them and their setting. "One of the main contributions of sociology," he asserted, lies "in the awareness that there is a close kinship among all these highly diverse [social] facts which have up to now been studied . . . in complete mutual independence." Each social fact, he felt, must be related "to a particular social milieu, to a definite type of society." [18] To do otherwise, he said, is to leave social facts—the facts of religion, law, moral ideas, and economics—"suspended in the void." To understand them is impossible, he held, "unless they are seen in their relations to each other and the collective milieu in the midst of which they develop and whose expression they are." [19]

Durkheim, no less than Spencer, considered societies as such to be important units of sociological analysis. He spoke of sociology as "the science of societies," [20] and repeatedly emphasized the importance of studying different types of society comparatively. Thus, he said: "One cannot explain a social fact of any complexity except by following its complete development through all social species. Comparative sociology is not a particular branch of sociology; it is sociology itself." [21]

Max Weber (1864–1920) devoted the greater part of his observations on sociology as a discipline to expounding the special method he advocated, called the method of understanding (verstehen)[22] and to discussing the vicissitudes of maintaining objectivity and neutrality of value judgments in social science. He did, however, offer a general definition of sociology which, incidentally, he referred to as "this highly ambiguous word." Sociology, according to Weber, "is a science which attempts the interpretive under-

[17] Émile Durkheim, *De La Méthode dans Les Sciences* (Paris: Alcan, 1902), p. 272.

[18] Durkheim, "Prefaces to L'Année Sociologique," in Wolff (ed.), *Émile Durkheim*.

[19] Durkheim, "Sociology," in Wolff (ed.), *Émile Durkheim*.

[20] Durkheim, "The Dualism of Human Nature and Its Social Conditions," in Wolff (ed.), *Émile Durkheim*, p. 326.

[21] Émile Durkheim (G. Catlin, ed.; S. Solovay and J. Mueller, trans.), *The Rules of Sociological Method*, 8th ed. (Chicago: University of Chicago Press, 1938), p. 139.

[22] Weber meant that sociologists must study social action by interpreting the motivational processes of the actors in their situational, historic, or symbolic contexts. It means, essentially, putting onself, in imagination, in the place of the other and, through intuition, coming to understand his action.

standing of social action in order thereby to arrive at a causal explanation of its course and effects." [23]

From our point of view, the crucial words in this definition are "social action." To that term Weber assigned a very broad meaning indeed, including "all human behavior when and in so far as the acting individual attaches a subjective meaning to it." [24] This might suggest that Weber regarded the "social act" or the "social relationship" as the particular subject matter of sociology. Weber did in fact propose an elaborate system for classifying social acts and social relationships, but he did not study them as such. He did not develop his sociology as a body of descriptive statements about such acts or the patterns of their relationship, nor did he offer any detailed explanations for such patterns. Instead, he addressed himself mainly to the analysis of concrete institutions. The subjects on which he wrote extensively include: religion; various aspects of economic life, including money and the division of labor; political parties and other forms of political organization and authority; bureaucracy and other varieties of large-scale organization; class and caste; the city; and music.

Neither the definition of sociology offered by Weber, nor the list of subjects on which he wrote, adequately expresses some of the most salient features of his work. His recent intellectual biographer, Professor Reinhard Bendix, says of Weber's justly famous studies of religion: "his three main themes were to examine the effect of religious ideas on economic activities, to analyze the relation between social stratification and religious ideas, and to ascertain and explain the distinguishing characteristics of Western civilization." [25] The first of these two themes we will immediately recognize as another instance of the conception of sociology as a discipline uniquely concerned with interrelations between the parts or elements of society. And the third theme, on the distinguishing characteristics of Western civilization, we must acknowledge to be another reference to that comparative sociology which treats societies as its unit of analysis and inquires into those factors which account for the similarities and differences between them as they exist in different places and times.

Although they by no means expressed themselves in precisely the same terms, the four founding fathers we consulted seem in basic agreement about the proper subject matter of sociology. First, all would allow, and in some cases would urge, sociologists to study a wide range of institutions, from the family to the state. These are to be analyzed in their own right, from the distinctive perspective of sociology, a perspective we have not yet fully defined. Second, those who define the classical tradition seem agreed that a unique subject matter for sociology is found in the interrelations among different institutions. Third, they concur in the opinion that society as a whole can be taken as a distinctive unit of sociological analysis, with sociology assigned the task of explaining wherein and why societies are alike or different. Finally, we must note among the classical writers in the field some sentiment in favor of focusing sociology on "social acts" or "social

[23] Max Weber (A. Henderson and T. Parsons, trans.), *Theory of Social and Economic Organization* (New York: Oxford University Press, 1947), p. 88.

[24] *Loc. cit.*

[25] Reinhard Bendix, *Max Weber: An Intellectual Portrait* (New York: Doubleday, 1960), p. 265 ff.

relationships" regardless of their institutional setting.[26] This view was most clearly expressed by Weber, but was voiced by other writers in the classical tradition as well.

What Sociologists Do

If we take "what sociologists do" as our guide to what sociology is about, there are three main sources we should examine: (1) the textbooks in which sociologists attempt to sum up their field, (2) the affiliations they choose when asked to identify themselves with one or another branch of sociology, and (3) the research they undertake and the reports they present at sociological meetings or publish in books and in their scholarly journals. All three approaches perhaps tend to reflect mainly what "average" or "typical" sociologists do. There are those who would say that whatever the average sociologist is doing, he *ought* to be doing something quite different. But let us for the moment withhold evaluation, to learn what the average sociologist, for good or ill, is actually doing.

Sociological Textbooks[27]

All but a small portion of the nation's sociologists teach, and the great majority teach from textbooks. These books present a basic conception of the field, and their use presumably reflects their acceptance by the profession. Between 1952 and 1958, 24 introductory textbooks on sociology were published in the United States. The single most popular text apparently was used by only about 15 per cent of the students enrolled in introductory sociology courses, and only two others captured as much as 10 per cent or more of the audience. Considering this wide diffusion, it becomes especially important in understanding the character of the field to know whether these texts reveal substantial agreement on the subject matter of sociology, or whether the diversity of point of view was as great as so large a number of texts might suggest.

Professor Hornell Hart, who analyzed the content of these textbooks, identified 12 themes which were dealt with within at least 20—that is, in almost 85 per cent of those he examined. The 12 leaders were: scientific method in sociology; personality in society; culture; human groups; population; caste and class; race; social change; economic institutions; family; education; and religion. Certain social processes did not make the top of the list largely because of the scoring scheme used. For example, if urban and rural life had not been treated separately, it is obvious that "community life" would have been cited by at least 20 out of 24 texts. Much the same may be said of the topic "social problems." In addition, a few obvious institutions came very close to making the top of the list, such as government and politics.

There seems substantial agreement on the dozen or so subjects which should be included in any introduction to sociology. Such agreement does not necessarily extend to the relative *importance* of different themes. On this issue the disagreement among sociologists probably far exceeds that which would probably be found in any of the natural sciences. Some of the texts differ in emphasis and from the average to such a degree that they give

[26] Social acts and social relationships are defined and discussed in some detail in Chap. 5.

[27] The bulk of the factual material presented in this description of the textbooks is drawn from an unpublished study by Professor Hornell Hart, Director of the Project for Comparative Analysis of Recent Introductory Sociologies, Florida Southern College.

a markedly different impression of what sociology is about. Thus, Professor Arnold Green's text[28] fails entirely to mention the following terms in either table of contents or index: attitudes, organizations, association, social control, crowds, public opinion, and social planning. Professor George Lundberg[29] assigns three times the average space to the topic "scientific methodology" and more or less ignores the subject of social control. Professor Ronald Freedman and his associates at the University of Michigan[30] allot almost three times as much space as does the average text to the topic of human ecology and community life, but almost totally neglect the themes of social interaction and communication.

Despite these important differences, the facts indicate that sociology has more of a common core than many people—including many sociologists—had believed to be the case. Weighing all his evidence, Professor Hart concluded: "There appears to be a solid and fairly definable core of sociological subject matter which is dealt with to a greater or lesser extent by almost all the text books."[31]

Sociologists Define Their "Field of Competence"

Not everyone will be too impressed by the evidence of basic agreement on subject matter in introductory sociology textbooks. Some would argue that the texts may cover the same themes only because experience has taught that these are the subjects which students most want to hear about. That might be said of race relations, but it can hardly be said of a topic such as scientific methodology, which is also a standard theme in texts. In any event, some will feel that neither the audience of beginning students nor the authors who write textbooks for them are the best authority for deciding what a field is about. They want to know how the profession as a whole defines its subject matter. Fortunately this is relatively easy to ascertain on the basis of studies conducted by the American Sociological Association.[32]

In 1950, and then again in 1959, each member of the Sociological Association was asked to list three sociological fields in which he felt qualified to teach or to do research. Each sociologist was free to describe his competence in his own terms, so that the categories which emerged were not predetermined. The individual responses were then sorted and grouped in 33 sets which seemed effectively to encompass all the fields mentioned. To a striking degree, the topics cited by the profession as a whole coincide with the 54 themes mentioned by one third or more of sociology textbooks.

There are, nevertheless, a few instances in which the lists do not completely coincide. Thus, the textbooks may have sections on government, politics, international relations, and war, but as a rule they do not sys-

[28] Arnold Green, *Sociology—An Analysis of Life in Modern Society*, 2nd ed. (New York: McGraw-Hill, 1956).

[29] George A. Lundberg, Clarence C. Schrag, and Otto N. Larsen, *Sociology*, rev. ed. (New York: Harper, 1958).

[30] Ronald Freeman, *et al., Principles of Sociology: A Text with Readings*, rev. ed. (New York: Holt, 1956).

[31] Hornell Hart, "Comparative Coverage on Agreed on Sociological Topics," *Third Report for the Project for Comparative Analysis of Introductory Sociology Textbooks*, 1959, p. 10.

[32] Matilda White Riley, "Membership in the American Sociological Association, 1950–1959," *American Sociological Review* (1960), XXV:914–926. The membership of the Association is more fully described in Chap. 8.

tematically discuss the sociology of knowledge, of history, and of law, which were cited as fields of competence in the poll of the sociologists. Since each of these fields was chosen by only 1 or 2 per cent of the sociologists, it might be argued that the matter is not serious. Many sociologists, however, will note with regret that contemporary textbooks do not give more attention to subjects which have figured so importantly in the history of sociological thought and research. Nevertheless, we may conclude that the profession as a whole identifies much the same range of topics as being of sociological interest as do the writers of textbooks.

In addition, these two sources agree quite closely in the relative *emphasis* they assign to the different sub-fields. This may be assessed by the proportion of all sociologists who select any particular topic as an area for specialization. At the top of the list are those subjects with which we have already become familiar: culture, psychological aspects of social life, marriage and the family, methodology, race and ethnic relations, and communication and opinion are among the fields in which the largest numbers of sociologists claim competence. The outstanding case of discrepancy involves "sociological theory" and "general sociology," which are among the fields most important to the profession but are not often treated as a separate topic in texts for beginners.

One can, of course, cite numerous reasons why we would be well-advised not to accept this approach as providing a definitive answer to what sociology is about. What sociologists are doing today may not reflect the traditional and continuing central concerns of sociology as a discipline. As an example we may cite the startlingly rapid growth of interest in the sociology of medicine. Before World War II there were not more than a dozen or so Americans working in the sociology of medicine; by 1960 there were several hundred so engaged. Between 1950 and 1959 medical sociology experienced a greater proportionate increase in adherents than any other sociological sub-field, the number claiming competence in it rising sevenfold in that period. Inevitably a special section devoted to this subject was formed within the American Sociological Association, thus placing it on an equal footing with some of the oldest of the more traditional sub-fields.

The increase in research on health and hospitals may perhaps be explained by the fact that the Congress of the United States created a new National Institute of Health, which was given a generous budget for research. The sociological study of illness and medicine became both more feasible and more attractive.

Not all the changes in sociological interest can be explained so easily. Second only to medical sociology in its rate of growth between 1950 and 1959 was the field of stratification, which also increased sevenfold. In this case it can hardly be claimed that a great outpouring of foundation or government research funds accounts for the greater interest in the study of social classes and social mobility. On the contrary, the increased importance of this topic must be recognized as a spontaneous growth of interest in a fundamental aspect of all societies which in the recent past had been unfortunately neglected. Guardians of the classical tradition in sociology may also take encouragement from the fact that among the other fields which gained adherents at a rate far above the average were: the sociology of law, religion, art, organization, and work.

On the whole, however, the relative attractiveness of different fields as subjects for specialization remained remarkably stable in the decade from 1950 to 1960. Of the 16 most popular fields in 1950, all but one (rural sociology) were among the top 16 nine years later. There were, in addition, very few dramatic changes in rank order, the most spectacular being the rise of social organization (including the study of social structure, institutions, leadership, and comparative institutional structure) from 16th place to 4th place. Among the top 16, the average change in rank order, however, was less than 2 places.

The Test of Elite Preference

It might be objected that the preferences and abilities of the rank and file of sociologists are interesting, but should not be assigned too much importance. To understand the central concerns of a discipline, one should look more to the leaders, the elite which sets the tone and determines by its influence the shape and direction of work which the rest follow.

Just who are the elite is not always easy to determine, and even when they have been identified they do not always make their position fully explicit. Perhaps we may agree that one group clearly belonging to the elite are those who play the leading role in shaping the program of the annual sociological meetings, and those who publish the materials appearing in leading sociological journals. In 1957 the sociological meetings were devoted to a broad review of the "Problems and Prospects of Sociology." The survey was designed to deal with all "the major branches of sociology." With the guidance of a Special Program Committee[33] some 30 sociological specialties were selected and studied, and the results later were assembled in a widely used book called *Sociology Today.*[34]

The now familiar topics all appear again: sociological theory, methodology, the individual in society, the family, the community, ethnic and race relations, and so on. There are a few important omissions, such as historical and military sociology—which the editors explicitly state were omitted only for lack of space. There are some signs of the rise to prominence of new fields—such as "the sociology of mental illness." On the whole, however, the choice of topics follows the pattern we have already discussed.

The fact that the 1957 meetings of the American Sociological Society were not unrepresentative of the interests of the most active sociologists can be verified by examining the distribution, by subject, of the articles they wrote for leading sociological journals. Although there are differences in emphasis according to the special interests of the various journals, in those devoted to general sociology, the familiar themes predominate. In the *American Sociological Review* in 1959, for example, the leading topics were social control and deviance, differentiation and stratification, scientific methodology, and so on down the list of themes we have already encountered.[35]

The Fields of Sociological Concern

Textbooks for introductory sociology courses, the rank-and-file membership of the American Sociological Association, and the leaders of the profession, all seem in basic agreement about the topics which

[33] The committee was headed by Professor Robert K. Merton of Columbia University, who was President of the Association for that year, and on whose initiative the theme for the year was selected.

[34] Robert K. Merton, Leonard Broom, and Leonard S. Cottrell, Jr. (eds.), *Sociology Today: Problems and Prospects* (New York: Basic Books, Inc., 1959), 599 pp.

[35] The distribution of articles in the Review was made on the basis of the scheme presented in Table 1.

constitute the subject matter of sociology. We can, therefore, construct a general outline of the fields of sociology on which almost everyone would agree.

Table 1

A General Outline of the Subject Matter of Sociology *

I. Sociological Analysis
  - Human Culture and Society
  - Sociological Perspective
  - Scientific Method in Social Science

II. Primary Units of Social Life
  - Social Acts and Social Relationships
  - The Individual Personality
  - Groups (including Ethnic and Class)
  - Communities: Urban and Rural
  - Associations and Organizations
  - Populations
  - Society

III. Basic Social Institutions
  - The Family and Kinship
  - Economic
  - Political and Legal
  - Religious
  - Educational and Scientific
  - Recreational and Welfare
  - Aesthetic and Expressive

IV. Fundamental Social Processes
  - Differentiation and Stratification
  - Cooperation, Accommodation, Assimilation
  - Social Conflict (including Revolution and War)
  - Communication (including Opinion Formation, Expression, and Change)
  - Socialization and Indoctrination
  - Social Evaluation (the Study of Values)
  - Social Control
  - Social Deviance (Crime, Suicide, etc.)
  - Social Integration
  - Social Change

* Some of the terms used in this chart are not self-explanatory. They are defined and discussed more fully at later points in this book, especially in Chaps. 5 and 6.

It is doubtful if very many sociologists would challenge any item on the list as not deserving its position. There are possibly one or two subjects which a substantial number of sociologists would regard as major omissions, but in most cases it could be shown that they are included in some other category. This is not to say that the list is exhaustive, far from it. Sociology has a tendency to break down into a seemingly endless list of specialties. Not only is there a sociology of small groups, but in some departments separate courses are given on "the two-man group." There is not only a general sociology of organization, there is also a special sociology of the hospital. There is a special and well-developed sociology of the stranger, and sociologists have even written on sociology of the bicycle. But these may all be seen as special cases and refinements of more general categories of sociological concern, about the inclusion of which there is general agreement. We must keep in mind, however, that the general agreement about the appropriateness of these topics as subjects of sociological interest would not necessarily extend to an evaluation of their relative importance, nor to judgments about how to study them.

What Reason Suggests

We might reasonably argue that neither what the founding fathers proposed, nor what sociologists today do is most appropriate for determining the proper subject matter of sociology. It should perhaps be decided by a process of logical analysis. Yet, as we will soon discover, just what is the most "logical" ground for allocating responsibility for the study of human affairs is far from self-evident.

Each of the social and humanistic branches of learning seems to have its distinctive subject matter. Political science, for example, deals with the ways in which society allocates the right to use legitimate power. It analyzes ideas about government and authority, and describes the actual distribution of public power and responsibility and the institutions through which it is exercised. Following this lead, our task becomes the simple one of finding for sociology some special or distinctive subject matter, preferably something concrete, specific, and easily identified, which is not claimed as the central object of study of some other established discipline.

The most cursory glance at the easily identified major institutions, social products, and processes reveals that there are indeed such unassigned or unclaimed subjects. Politics and economics are spoken for, and so in large measure are literature, language, education, and business. But there remain the family, crime, social classes, ethnic and racial groups, the urban and the rural community. No one of these major components of society has become the distinctive object of study for a specialized branch of learning having the status of an independent discipline comparable to politics or economics. Instead, each of these subjects has become a focus for research and theory-building within sociology. In this way sociology has, to a degree, become the great residual category of the social sciences. It has not one subject, but many. Indeed, some might argue, that in this sense sociology has no *distinctive* subject matter. It is merely a congeries of disciplines united mainly by the fact that they deal with institutions and social processes which have historically failed to become sufficiently specialized and important to win independent standing as intellectual disciplines.

At any time, of course, any one of these sub-fields may yet be established as a separate discipline, providing the basis for departments in universities and becoming recognized as an independent field by learned academies, foundations, and the scholarly community as a whole. To some extent this has already happened to the study of population and demography, to criminology and penology, to industrial sociology, and to the study of the family.

If the long continuing process of differentiation and specialization in scholarship were to go so far that all the sub-fields of sociology came to be established as separate disciplines, would sociology then cease to exist as a discipline in its own right? We can properly say "no" only if we can point to a distinctive subject matter which would remain for sociology. Happily we can. Indeed, aided by the analysis in the preceding sections of this chapter, we may propose several distinctive subject matters to which sociology could still lay claim. They are, in decreasing order of size and complexity: societies, institutions, and social relationships.

Sociology as the Study of Society

Sociology need not be the study of any one part, it may be the study of the whole—that is, sociology may be a special discipline which takes society as its unit of analysis. Its purpose then would be to discover how the institutions which make up a society are related to one another in different social systems. The specialist in government may study types of government, asking how the legislative, judicial, and administrative functions are allocated, how the units which perform these functions are related to one another, what consequences follow from centralizing administration while leaving the legislative power diffuse. Just so, there may be a branch of learning which concentrates on society as the unit of analysis. Such a study of society would have at least two main divisions, one more concerned with the internal differentiation of particular societies, the other treating all societies as a population having certain identifiable external characteristics. In the latter case, sociology would ask questions of the following type: Is there any evidence that particular types of society, say the great empires, tend to endure for any specific period of time? Do societies go through definite stages of development? Questions of this order once dominated sociological thought, especially in the form of the evolutionary theory of social development.[36] The discrediting of the evolutionary theories tended to discourage further efforts along this line.

Currently much more popular, and apparently successful, are those studies of society which inquire mainly into its internal structure. Typical questions asked in this tradition are: What are the internal problems which any society must face? What are the most common components found in most societies? How do societies typically allocate responsibility for various functions? What are the consequences of combining certain institutions—for example, how compatible is the industrial pattern of economic life with the "extended" household type of family?

A great deal of what is often called historical and comparative sociology follows this pattern. In one of the classic series of studies undertaken by Max Weber, he posed this set of questions: Does not each religious ethic contain implications for action in the real world, especially for man's economic action? And in so far as this is true, would it not follow that the communicants of certain religions would be more active or effective in economic life than those following different religious ethics? Weber pursued these questions through an imposing series of studies of the influence of religion on economic activity in China, India, and Protestant Europe, in the last instance producing one of the best known and controversial studies of all social science in *The Protestant Ethic and the Spirit of Capitalism.* We cite Weber as an example of the study of society because his interest was not in religion as such, but rather in the effect which particular types of religious organization had on other aspects of social life, in particular, on economic life.

Sociology as the Study of Institutions

The idea that the distinctive unit of sociological analysis is society, more specifically the relations between the elements which compose it, is old and widely held. It can be argued, however, that institu-

[36] This evolutionary theory is fully discussed in Chap. 3.

tions as such—the family, the church, the school, and the political party—are a more distinctive subject matter for sociology, because society as a whole is already the unit of analysis in the fields of history and anthropology. The questions which would be dealt with by a special discipline devoted to institutions are of this order: What features do all institutions have in common? What are the dimensions on which they are distinguishable, and how do these dimensions vary when one compares institutions that perform different functions? Regardless of their function, do institutions come to share certain other features by virtue of being alike in size, in degree of specialization, in amount of autonomy, and so on?

Durkheim, as long ago as 1901, said that sociology "can be defined as the science of institutions,"[37] but this form of sociological analysis has not been intensively developed. The growing importance in the modern world of one type of institution, the large-scale organization, has, however, led to renewed interest in and research on the general properties of institutions.

Sociology as the Study of Social Relationships

Just as societies are complex systems of institutions, so institutions may be conceived of as complex systems of still simpler "social relationships." The family, for example, is made up of many sets of relationships—those between man and woman, parent and child, brother and sister, grandparent and grandchild. Each of these may be studied as a particular type of relationship. And in all relationships, we can pursue certain common emphases, involving such attributes as the size of the group (dyad, triad, etc.), or the quality of the relationship—as, for example, in the study of dominance and submission.

On analytic grounds we may argue that such relationships form a distinctive subject matter, and that just as the common and differentiating properties of institutions can be studied in and of themselves, so one could study social relationships in the same way. Going even further, we might argue that such relationships are merely the "molecules" of social life, and that there is still a smaller unit, the "social act," the true "atom" of social life, which could be the special subject matter of sociology.

We will discuss the meaning of these terms more fully in a later chapter. For now we merely note that Max Weber took quite seriously the idea that sociology might be mainly a study of social relationships and acts, and elaborated a set of categories for their description and analysis. Other leading German sociologists shared this perspective. Leopold von Wiese argued at length in favor of treating social relationships as the only truly distinctive subject matter of sociology,[38] and much of the sociological writing of Georg Simmel[39] was an application of this principle. Among contemporary sociologists, Talcott Parsons has expressed similar views.[40] Systematic empirical research focused on the social act and the social relationship has, however, only recently been done on any substantial scale, mainly in the study of small groups and in industrial research.

[37] Durkheim, *The Rules of Sociological Method*, p. lvi.

[38] Leopold von Wiese (F. H. Mueller, ed. and ann.), *Sociology* (New York: Piest, 1941), and (adapted and amplified by Howard Becker), *Systematic Sociology on the Basis of the Beziehungslehre and Gebeldelehre of Leopold von Wiese* (New York: Wiley, 1932), 772 pp..

[39] Georg Simmel (Kurt H. Wolff, ed. and trans.), *The Sociology of Georg Simmel* (Glencoe, Ill.: The Free Press, 1950).

[40] Talcott Parsons, *The Social System* (Glencoe, Ill.: The Free Press, 1951).

Proceeding on the principle that each discipline should have a distinctive subject matter, we found that series of institutions which failed to become the subject of any established discipline have instead become sub-fields of sociology. We have seen, as well, that even if institutions such as the family were to become the subject matter of separately established disciplines, still, societies, institutions, social relationships, and social processes such as differentiation, co-operation, evalution, and competition would remain as distinctive foci for sociological analysis. Of course, anthropology also deals with all these subjects, and history also concerns itself with societies and institutions. To discriminate precisely between any two fields, we must consider not only their subject matter but their goals and methods. We therefore leave further distinctions between sociology, history, and anthropology to our next chapter.

In this chapter, we explored three different paths leading to a delineation of the subject matter of sociology, considering in turn: "What the founding fathers said," "what sociologists do," and "what logic requires." All three approaches indicate that sociology deals with a wide range of institutions and social processes. Sociology's claim to some of these poses no particular problem. It is unthinkable that an institution so ubiquitous as the family or a process so critical as social stratification should not be the object of intensive and specialized study. Sociology may then be seen as a collection of sub-disciplines dealing with institutions and social processes not claimed by more specialized disciplines.

Yet we must recognize that even when institutions such as the economic and political are the subject of specialized and independent branches of scholarship, they nevertheless continue to be objects of sociological investigation. This is not mere redundancy nor scholarly imperialism. The aspect of any institution or social process which links it to any other is its character as an interlocking "system" of action.[41] We can, therefore, say that *sociology is the study of systems of social action and of their interrelations.* Most prominent among these systems of action we find, in increasing order of size and complexity: single social acts, social relationships, organizations and institutions, communities and societies.[42]

This was not immediately apparent to us from the study of textbooks, because we could there tell only which institutions were discussed, and not what aspect of them was emphasized. Looking back now at the subjects in which sociologists feel themselves competent, we may recall that among the most frequently cited specialties were "theory" and "general sociology." We did not earlier explore the meaning of those terms. If we had, we would have discovered that by these choices many sociologists were expressing their opinion that *sociology is not merely a collection of sub-disciplines on all realms of life, but rather is the study of those aspects of social life which are present in all social forms.* This idea was, of course, often made explicit in the sociological classics. One also inevitably encounters it if one seeks by logical analysis to delineate a distinctive subject matter for sociology which does not conflict with the claims of disciplines focused on particular institutions such as the political and the economic.

To understand sociology we obviously need to know something about the subject matter. But even more fundamental in defining the character of any discipline are the questions it asks about its subject matter and the

[41] "Systems of action" are more fully discussed in Chap. 5.

[42] These terms are defined and more fully discussed in Chap. 5.

ways in which it goes about answering them. Lists of subjects, such as have been presented in Table 1 tell us what sociology deals with without quite answering the question: "What is sociology all about?" We are, so far, in the position of a student who is sent off to write a paper on human biology as a branch of science and returns to report that it is the study of arms, legs, heads, and the like; that it also deals with circulation, breathing, and digestion; and that in addition it compares men and women. Such information is certainly something to go by, but it hardly defines the field.

We must yet discover what is the particular perspective in which sociology sees these subjects, how it approaches them, what methods of inquiry it utilizes, and what order of conclusion it draws from its investigation. These are the themes which will concern us in the chapters which follow. In them it will become apparent that some of the differences in emphasis to which we have so far only alluded in elucidating the subject matter of sociology become quite important when decisions must be reached about the relative emphasis to give various subjects and about the methods for investigating them.

two

the sociological perspective

In this chapter we address ourselves to two tasks: to clarify the relation of sociology to the other disciplines which deal with man in society, and to offer a more formal definition of sociology. Both represent unfinished business carried over from the preceding chapter. Our analysis of these issues, taken together, presents a conception of what is distinctive in the sociological perspective.

We earlier made quite explicit our position that the subject matter of sociology could not in itself serve to define the field. We need not pause long, therefore, to justify our attempt at a more formal definition of the essential features of sociological analysis. The relation of sociology to other disciplines is another matter. Intellectual disciplines are so complex and diverse that any brief effort to characterize them must necessarily be full of arbitrary and even distorted images. When we attempt to discriminate between the branches of social study, the temptation is inevitably great to exaggerate differences rather than to acknowledge similarities. Despite these grave risks, we clearly must offer some map of the terrain to those who wish to orient themselves in the complex realm of the social sciences. First, and necessarily superficial, impressions may be altered as the novice becomes better oriented and deepens his understanding of social science. And it is important to recognize that the differences in the perspective and practice of the several disciplines which treat man in society are often fundamental and have endured for relatively long periods of time.

Sociology and Related Disciplines

Sociology is a behavioral science. It seeks to explain contemporary or past human behavior as we experience it directly or encounter it embodied in artifacts, monuments, laws, and books. But in this sense history, economics, and even literary criticism are also behavioral sciences. Some grasp of what is distinctive about the sociological approach to these phenomena is necessary to our understanding of what sociology is.

The learned community is no tight ship all neatly divided into separate water-tight compartments of knowledge. Any effort to distinguish sociology from other disciplines must be somewhat arbitrary and imprecise. As knowledge advances and trends of research change, currently adequate definitions of the several social sciences will be rendered inaccurate. Viewing the problem from a historical perspective, Professor Joseph J. Schwab, philosopher and historian of science, reports that "A mode of inquiry discredited by one scientist, dismissed at one time, discarded in one science, reappears and is fruitful in other hands and other times, or in other sciences." [1] Nevertheless, the branches of study concerned with man and his work do reveal numerous distinguishing features which, at the present time, fairly clearly mark off one discipline from another. Among the critical questions we ask as a basis for characterizing these disciplines is whether they are multi-dimensional or focus on only one aspect of social life, and if so which one; whether they are directly concerned with the observation of behavior or concentrate on data further removed from the realm of everyday action; whether they assign a prime role to abstract theory and generalization or emphasize description of the immediate and the concrete; and whether they stress measurement and mathematical manipulation of data or favor direct observation and a more "clinical" or "empathetic" mode of understanding human action. Since the same questions can equally well be put to all the disciplines, they do not suggest a natural order or presentation. I have, therefore, chosen to describe first those which are least likely to be confused with sociology—namely, economics, political science, and history—and then those less easily distinguished from sociology—namely, psychology and anthropology.

Economics is sometimes called "the dismal science," a fact in which sociologists take some comfort whenever their discipline is dubbed "the painful elaboration of the obvious." Whatever comic relief this exchange of insults may give, it does not suffice to distinguish between economics and sociology as behavioral sciences.

Economics is the study of the production and distribution of goods and services. As it developed in the Western World, largely under the influence of the Classical School in England, economics has dealt almost exclusively with the interrelations of purely economic variables: the relations of price and supply, money flows, input-output ratios, and the like. Relatively little attention has been paid to the individual's actual economic behavior or motivation, and only modest energy has gone into studying productive enterprises as social organizations. This left great gaps in our knowledge of economic life. More important, it left the discipline inadequate to account for the actual course of economic events. Recently economists have shown more interest in motivation and in the institutional context of economic action. Nevertheless, many important problems, highly relevant to economics, have not yet become the object of concentrated economic research. Studies of the role of values and preferences in affecting the supply of labor, the influence

[1] Joseph J. Schwab, "What Do Scientists Do?", *Behavioral Science* (1960), V:1.

exerted by prestige or custom on the price of goods, the origins and motivations of entrepreneurs and managers, and the contribution of education to productivity have been largely left to sociologists and psychologists. Only a few hardy economists have ventured to deal with them.

The restriction of the economists' horizon is certainly a source of weakness, but it has had its advantages in facilitating the development of economics as a highly focused, coherent discipline of considerable intellectual accomplishment. Sociologists often envy the economists for the precision of their terminology, the exactness of their measures, the ease with which they can communicate with one another in a standard technical language, the extent of their agreement about certain basic principles, and their ability to translate the results of their theoretical work into practical suggestions having major implications for public policy. On the other hand, the economists' record in predicting economic events is very imperfect indeed, presumably because they fail to give due weight to factors such as individual motivation and institutional resistance, which the sociologist feels well-qualified to study.

The parallels between the structure of economic and sociological thinking are, nevertheless, many and striking. Most modern sociologists find the economist's way of thinking more congenial than that of the historian or the political theorist.[2] Economists think, as do sociologists, in terms of systems and sub-systems; they stress the relations between parts, especially patterns of dependence, dominance, exchange, and the like. Both are interested in measurement, often precise, and in relationships between sets of variables. Both are impressed with mathematical models as aids in analyzing data.[3]

Political science, or "government," as it is taught in most American universities, consists mainly of two elements: political theory and government administration. Neither branch involves extensive contact with political behavior. Courses in political theory usually examine ideas about government from Plato through Machiavelli and Rousseau to Marx. Courses on administration generally describe the formal structure and functions of government agencies, but less often deal in intimate detail with their actual operation.

Sociology is devoted to the study of all aspects of society, whereas political science restricts itself mainly to the study of power as embodied in formal organizations. Sociology stresses the interrelations between sets of institutions including government, whereas political science tends to turn its attention inward to the processes *within* government. Nevertheless, political sociology long shared with political science many of the same interests and a very similar style of work. Certain figures, important to sociologists but not to political science, such as Max Weber or Robert Michels, played a more important role in courses in political sociology. There were, in addition, some differences in emphasis. In S. M. Lipset's words: "Political science has been concerned with *public administration*, or how to make governmental organizations efficient; political sociology, on the other hand, has been interested in *bureaucracy*, particularly in the specification of its inherent stresses and strains." [4] In spite of this, the content and emphasis in courses on political theory were much the same whether they were listed in the catalogue as courses in government or in political sociology.

[2] For example, see Talcott Parsons and Neil Smelser, *Economy and Society: A Study in the Integration of Economics and Social Theory* (Glencoe, Ill.: The Free Press, 1956).

[3] See the discussion of mathematical models in sociology in Chap. 7.

[4] S. Martin Lipset, "Political Sociology," in Robert K. Merton, Leonard Broom, and Leonard S. Cottrell, Jr. (eds.), *Sociology Today: Problems and Prospects* (New York: Basic Books, 1959), p. 83. Italics in original.

In the last 30 years, however, sociologists interested in politics have differentiated themselves from political scientists through an intensive program of research on political *behavior*.[5] They vigorously investigated voting behavior, popular attitudes and values about political issues, the membership of radical political movements on both the left and right, voluntary organizations, and the process of decision-making within small communities and inside large private and governmental bureaucracies.[6] This gave political sociology a new character which marks it clearly as a branch of behavioral science. Some political scientists are also turning more actively to behavioral studies of politics, notably the late V. O. Key at Harvard, Robert Dahl at Yale, and Gabriel Almond at Stanford.[7] In their work the distinction between a sociological and a political analysis breaks down, and a new behavioral science of political processes emerges.

History seeks to establish the sequence in which events occurred; it is the arrangement of behavior in time. Sociologists are much more concerned to show the relationships between events occurring more or less at the same time. Historians, almost by definition, restrict themselves to study of the past, often the more distant the better. Sociologists show much more interest in the contemporary scene or the recent past. Historians, with the notable exception of those called "philosophers of history," as a rule eschew the exploration of causes; they are content to establish how things actually happened. Sociologists are much more likely to seek for the interrelations between events and to propose causal sequences. The historian prides himself on the explicitness, the concreteness of detail which characterizes his discipline. The sociologist is more likely to abstract from concrete reality, to categorize and generalize, to be interested in what is true not only of a particular people's history but of the histories of many different peoples. From the historian's perspective, this sociological process of abstracting from the history of several countries or periods is viewed as likely to distort the distinctive reality of some *one* historical place or period.

Much, perhaps most, of man's history has been written as the history of kings and wars. The history of less glamorous or exciting events, the changes through time in institutional forms such as landowning, or in social relations such as those of men and women in the family, have less frequently interested historians. Such relationships, however, lie at the center of the sociologists' concern.

[5] For example, see S. Martin Lipset in Robert K. Merton, Leonard Broom, and Leonard S. Cottrell, Jr. (eds.), *Sociology Today*, pp. 81–114; Alex Inkeles, "National Character and Modern Political Systems," in Francis Hsu (ed.), *Psychological Anthropology* (Homewood, Ill.: Dorsey, 1961), pp. 172–208; Feliks Gross, "Political Sociology," in Joseph S. Roucek (ed.), *Contemporary Sociology* (New York: Philosophical Library, 1958), pp. 201–223.

[6] Paul Lazarsfeld, Bernard Berelson, and Hazel Gaudet, *The People's Choice* (New York: Columbia University Press, 1944); Elihu Katz and Paul Lazarsfeld, *Personal Influence* (Glencoe, Ill., The Free Press, 1955); Hadley Cantril, *The Politics of Despair* (New York: Basic Books, 1958); S. Martin Lipset, Martin A. Trow, and James S. Coleman, *Unison Democracy* (Glencoe, Ill.: The Free Press, 1956); Oliver Garceau, *The Political Life of the American Medical Association* (Cambridge: Harvard University Press, 1941); William Kornhauser, *The Politics of Mass Society* (Glencoe, Ill.: The Free Press, 1959); Amitai Etzioni, A *Comparative Analysis of Complex Organizations* (Glencoe, Ill.: The Free Press, 1961).

[7] V. O. Key, Jr., *Southern Politics in State and Nation* (New York: Knopf, 1949); Robert Dahl and C. E. Lindbloom, *Politics, Economics, and Welfare: Planning and Politico-economic Systems Resolved into Basic Social Processes* (New York: Harper, 1953); Gabriel Almond, *The Appeals of Communism* (Princeton: Princeton University Press, 1954).

Despite these differences in emphasis, there are important bases for the concordance of history and sociology. Some historians, among them some of the greatest, such as Rostovtzev, G. G. Coulton, and Jacob Burkhardt,[8] have written *social* history—that is, history which deals with human relations, social patterns, mores and customs, and important institutions other than monarchy and army. And some of the most outstanding sociological analysis, as in the work of Max Weber, has been applied to historical problems. Sociologists acknowledge historical sociology as one of the standard special fields of their discipline, and Sigmund Diamond, Robert Bellah, and Norman Birnbaum may be pointed to as important contemporary practitioners.[9]

Psychology is often defined as the science of mind, or of mental processes. Its studies encompass the capacities of the mind to receive sensations, to give them meaning, and to respond to them. In other words, it deals with mental processes such as perception, cognition, and learning. Modern psychologists also devote particular attention to feelings and emotions, to motives as well as drives, and to their organization in what we call personality.

Psychology has deep roots in biology and physiology, and remains closely tied to them. Much of the research by psychologists on visual and aural perception has little relevance for social behavior. On the other hand, studies of emotion, cognition, motivation, and the like, have an intimate connection with the individual's participation in social relationships. Students of perception, learning, and other mental processes generally look for laws of psychic functioning which transcend the differences between individuals and even species. Those dealing with the emotions, feelings, and conative (striving) behavior are more often concerned with the individual and the distinctive or unique organization of his personality. This is particularly true of "clinical" psychologists.

For those psychologists more concerned with the psyche than with physiology, the term "personality" serves as a central organizing concept in much the same way as "society" and "social system" serve the sociologist.[10] Psychology, in this perspective, seeks to explain behavior as it is organized in an individual personality and determined by the combined influence of his physiology, his psychic apparatus, and his unique personal experience. By contrast, sociology attempts to understand behavior as it is organized in a society, and as it is determined by such factors as the number of people it contains, their culture, their objective situation, their social organization.

Sociology and psychology draw closest in the special field of social psychology. From the psychological point of view, social psychology is concerned with the ways in which personality and behavior are influenced by a person's *social* characteristics or his social setting. As an example, we may cite Solomon Asch's studies of conformity and perception. In these studies he

[8] Mikhail I. Rostovtzev, *The Social and Economic History of the Hellenistic World* (Oxford: The Clarendon Press, 1941); George C. Coulton, *Medieval Panorama: The English Scene from Conquest to Reformation* (New York: Meridian Books, 1957); Jakob Burckhardt (S. G. C. Middlemore, trans.), *The Civilization of the Renaissance in Italy* Vol. I–II (New York: Harper, 1958).

[9] Sigmund Diamond, *The Reputation of the American Businessman* (Cambridge: Harvard University Press, 1955); Robert Bellah, *Tokugawa Religion: The Values of Pre-Industrial Japan* (Glencoe, Ill.: The Free Press, 1957); Norman Birnbaum, "Social Structure and the German University," (Ph.D. Thesis, Harvard University, 1958); "Great Britain: The Reactive Revolt," in M. Kaplan (ed.), *The Revolution in World Politics* (New York: Wiley, 1962). Also see George C. Homans, *English Villagers of the Thirteenth Century* (Cambridge: Harvard University Press, 1941).

[10] These concepts are defined and discussed in Chap. 5.

showed that people will report the length of a line as shorter or longer than it actually is, contradicting the evidence of their senses, if a majority of the other experimental subjects all connive at calling the line longer or shorter than they know it to be. Thus, Asch showed how a *psychic* process—perception—was influenced by a *social* situation—minority status—producing perceptual distortion.[11]

From a sociological perspective, social psychology includes any study of *social* processes which systematically considers how the psychological properties of every man, or the personality dispositions of particular men, acting in a situation, influence the outcome of the social process. Thus, Janowitz and Marvick, in their study of voting, demonstrated with a representative national sample of Americans, that favoring an isolationist foreign policy is more common not only among persons of limited education, but also among those with an authoritarian *personality* structure.[12] In this case, a rate of social action—the proportion voting isolationist—was shown to vary in response to the personality dispositions of the persons in the group.

The distinction between the sociological and the psychological perspective in social psychology often breaks down in the actual practice of research. In studies of public opinion, of mob action such as riots or lynchings, of mass movements in politics or religion, it is often difficult to see any difference in the work of those who were sociologically trained as against those trained in psychology. Indeed, many argue that social psychology should be recognized as a distinct field, much as biochemistry has been, and both the University of Michigan and Columbia University have established separate programs offering a degree in social psychology independent of the requirements in the sociology and psychology departments.

Anthropology, at least in the United States, is as diversified a subject as sociology, incorporating archeology, physical anthropology, cultural history, many branches of linguistics, and the study of all aspects of the life of primitive man everywhere. Like psychology, it has strong ties with the natural sciences, and in the case of physical anthropology, a close link with biology.

It is as the science of culture that anthropology is most germane to sociology. Culture may be defined narrowly, to mean mainly the system of symbols, including language and values, shared by a given people. In that case we consider anthropology to have a distinct subject matter in the same sense that we consider power and authority to be the subject matter of political science and the production and distribution of goods the distinctive subject matter of economics. But if culture is defined broadly to include all the patterned ways of doing things, including not only shared values but shared institutional arrangements, then anthropology becomes co-extensive with sociology. In fact, in British universities, anthropology was well-established as the academic study of society long before sociology was accepted, and in many American universities the two departments are combined.

Nevertheless, anthropology and sociology differ in that the former takes prime responsibility for studying primitive or non-literate man, the latter for studying more advanced civilizations. This basic fact exerts a pervasive influence on the content and subject matter of the two disciplines. Anthropologists tend to study societies in all their aspects, as wholes. In so far as they

[11] Solomon Asch, *Social Psychology* (Englewood Cliffs, N. J.: Prentice-Hall, 1952), pp. 450–501.

[12] Morris Janowitz and D. Marvick, "Authoritarianism and Political Behavior," *Public Opinion Quarterly* (1953), XVII:185–201.

specialize, it is usually in a given "culture area," such as Melanesia. Sociologists more often study parts of a society, and generally specialize in some institution such as the family, or a process, such as social mobility. Anthropologists traditionally live in the community they study, directly observing behavior or recording customs as reported by their informants. Their method of analysis is essentially qualitative and "clinical." Sociologists more often rely on statistics and questionnaires; their analysis is more often formal and quantitative. The natural milieu for the anthropologist is the small self-contained group or community, whereas the sociologist is quite at ease in studying large-scale and impersonal organizations and processes.

So long as there are distinctive indigenous peoples preserving their unique cultures, anthropologists will not lack for a special subject matter. Even if many of the people he studies move into the modern world, the anthropologist may follow comfortably along so long as "his" people maintain a distinctive community within the framework of the larger society. But as its traditional subjects become fully acculturated, and are dispersed throughout the larger society and absorbed within it, anthropology will be less able to survive as a distinctive discipline. It may become a branch of sociology specializing in the study of values or the small community; or it may be entirely absorbed, along with sociology, in a general science of society.

Disciplines, Boundaries, and Issues

Benjamin Kidd, writing about sociology in the 11th edition of *The Encyclopaedia Britannica,* said: "From the 17th century forward it may be said, strictly speaking, that all leading contributions to the general body of Western philosophy have been contributions to the science of society (sociology)." He went on to point out that over the years the following terms have been seriously proposed as substitutes for the word "sociology": politics, political science, social economy, social philosophy, and social science.[13] Under the circumstances, any novice in the field must surely be forgiven if he expresses some bewilderment when faced with the task of distinguishing one social science from another. Maintaining these distinctions is made more difficult by the readiness of sociologists to accept responsibility for any institution which is not already the subject of an established discipline. To the degree that these subjects are important and would otherwise be neglected, sociologists deserve more to be praised than criticized. The scholarly world has shown a remarkable capacity to exclude from serious study enormous ranges of human activity, as if the common human nature expressed in family life, in stratification, in crime, made these vulgar studies unfit subjects for gentlemen scholars. For a new branch of study to win recognition in the university and the learned academies has been only slightly less difficult than for the camel to pass through that gate in Jerusalem known as "the needle's eye."

This open quality of sociology, its ready acceptance of new topical fields, stems from the sociologist's general concern with systems of social action and their interrelations.[14] Inevitably this leads him to deal with all aspects of man's social life, whether or not the subject has already been marked out as the special province or preserve of some other discipline.

There is no court to which we can turn for the adjudication of such

[13] "Sociology," Vol. XXV, *Encyclopedia Britannica* (1911), p. 322 *ff*.

[14] Systems of social action are defined and discussed in Chap. 5.

territorial disputes. Of each intellectual discipline which takes a particular subject in hand we may inquire: Does it ask challenging questions? Is there, or can we devise, a method for exploring the questions it raises? Once applied, will this method yield meaningful facts? Can these facts be grouped together to formulate conclusions or generalizations which are contributions to knowledge? Do these conclusions now point the way to new questions which can carry us still further forward in our effort to understand man and his works? How, and how well, sociology meets these challenges we shall see in subsequent chapters. In the next section we seek the answer to the first question: What is the main issue to which sociology addresses itself?

Toward a Definition of Sociology: Social Order, Disorder, and Change

If you were to insist that the basic problem to which sociology addresses itself be described in a single phrase, we would reply: It seeks to explain the nature of social order and social disorder.

Sociology shares with all other essentially scientific perspectives the assumption that there is order in nature, and that it can be discovered, described, and understood. Just as the laws of physics describe the underlying order governing the relation of physical objects, astronomy the order of the planetary system, geology the order underlying the history and present structure of the earth, so sociology seeks to discover, describe, and explain the order which characterizes the social life of man.

When we speak of "order" we mean that events occur in a more-or-less regular sequence or pattern, so that we can make an empirically verifiable statement about the relation of one event to another at given points in time under specified conditions. Sociology deals with several such forms of order, varying greatly in scale but each having substantially the same character.

The problem is perhaps most evident at the level of the largest unit with which sociology usually deals, the nation-state or other form of large-scale society. Collectively, the members of a large society perform millions, or even billions, of social acts in the course of a single day.[15] Yet the outcome is not bedlam, total confusion and chaos, but rather a reasonable approximation of order. This order permits each individual to pursue his personal course without too seriously interfering with the pursuit by others of their purposes and goals. Indeed, this order generally assures that each can actually facilitate to some degree the attainment by others of their goals. The prime object of sociology is to explain how this comes about, how some reasonable degree of coordination of so many diverse individual actions yields the routine flow of social life. When we say that there is a social system, we refer to the coordination and integration of social acts which permit them to occur in a way that produces order rather than chaos.

Since our emphasis on order may be so easily misunderstood, we hasten to add early and emphatically that to delineate the nature of the social order is not necessarily to approve or justify it. A totalitarian government also develops a social order. A sociologist who studies it may explain the role of the monolithic party in monopolizing political power. He may show how the media of mass communication are used to mobilize public opinion and to manufacture the appearance of consensus, or expose the role which secret-police terror plays in permitting the elite to effect social control. In so doing,

[15] See Chap. 5 for definitions and discussions of the terms social act and society.

he obviously is not justifying, excusing, nor indeed in any necessary way judging the social order with which he deals. The sociologist may certainly be stimulated by his own values to explore and to emphasize one rather than another problem within such a system. In doing the job of analysis, he is also giving those of us not familiar with the system a basis on which we can form our own moral and political judgment. But such judgment should not be confused with the separate task of describing the basic order by which, for good or ill, a particular social system is kept in operation.

The sociologist's concern with the *problem* of order should not lead one to assume that he has no interest in or responsibility for studying manifestations of disorder. No social system functions flawlessly, regardless of the perspective from which it is viewed. Certainly no social system is perfect from the point of view of all its members. It is endemic in social life that some norms will not be met, some values not fulfilled, some goals not attained. Indeed, in any society, there may be some important realms in which the *majority* violate the socially or legally defined standard, and often at great cost of life. A trip along any of the highways of the United States during the Labor Day weekend will suffice to make the point. Almost all societies know periods, often long ones, of riot, civil war, mob violence, terror, crime, and general disorganization. Each of these manifestations is a departure from some social order already established or, as in case of counter-revolution, one seeking to establish itself. And even disorder is not necessarily chaos.

Within both individual and collective life there are "natural" forces making for order and stability and other equally "natural" forces making for disorder, conflict, and disruption. The balance between these forces may be very different at different times. It is a matter of preference, of personal inclination or philosophic orientation, whether you choose to see the world as a place inherently in a state of disorder struggling to achieve some order, or as normally in a condition of order but subject to constant disruption and the threat of disorder. For myself, I am quite satisfied that it fits the existing facts better, and is more conducive to effective analysis, to assume order as man's basic condition. To make this assumption is very far from passing on the importance of studying man's frequent and important plunges into a state of relative disorder. I stress "relative," because without some order, even within conditions of seeming general disorder, man would cease to survive. Some societies persistently failed to solve the problem of maintaining order, and have dissolved, their members scattered, absorbed elsewhere, or totally vanished. But always there has been another social system in which order prevailed and social man survived.

A sociology which completely ignores the manifestations of disorder in social life is clearly an incomplete and inadequate sociology. No less may be said of one which denies the basic facts of social order and turns its back on the mechanisms which insure it, concerning itself exclusively with the problems of social disorganization. The conflict between those who hold out for an "equilibrium theory" and those who urge us to adopt a "conflict theory" of society is sterile,[16] since a complete sociology must include both the study of order and disorder, and also of orderly and disorderly *change*. Arnold Feldman and Wilbert Moore urge on us the more dynamic, inclusive conception of society as a "tension management system."

"The 'order' characteristic of any social system thus consists of both regularized patterns of action and institutions that control, ameliorate, or

[16] These conceptions of society and their protagonists are discussed in Chap. 3.

canalize the conflict produced by persistent strains. A society encompasses conflict and its associated change as well as a social order that comprises tension-preventing and tension-managing devices and systems." [17]

To delineate the social system by defining the underlying relationships among a complex set of social acts is perhaps the prime responsibility of the sociologist, but it is obviously only a beginning. Indeed, some sociologists argue that it is less important than another task, that of accounting for the persistence of social systems through time. The coordination, at a single point in time, of thousands and even millions of individual acts in a more or less stable system of social action is perhaps miraculous. Yet this short-term order is only a minor wonder compared to the grand miracle represented by the persistence of such systems of action over relatively long periods of time. Groups of animals, including dogs and elephants, can be trained to coordinate their behavior in very complex patterns of action. Without their trainer, however, these animals have no way of passing on to subsequent generations the tricks they have learned. The complex coordination of human action which every social system represents is almost always carried forward through time beyond the lives of any single set of participants. Such continuity is also found in colonies of social insects, but in their case we know that instinct insures the appropriate outcome. Since instinctive regulation of behavior is not equally important in man, the continuity of the social order must be explained by reference to other mechanisms.

Sociology, then, seeks to explain the continuity of social systems through time. Yet continuity must be recognized as relative. Its occurrence cannot be taken as assured, but rather must be acknowledged to be problematic. There is reason to believe that some unusually stable societies continued unchanged in all essential respects, often down to the smallest detail, generation after generation, for perhaps hundreds of years. Our impression of the relatively unchanging nature of these societies may be mainly an artifact of the inadequacy of the historical record. In any event, most of the societies which form part of the more recent history of man seem to have experienced an almost continuous, often pervasive, and sometimes highly accelerated process of change. Yet with change, as with continuity, the sociologist assumes that the sequence of events is inherently orderly. The process of change is not random, even though it may at times seem chaotic, and is often beyond the conscious control of individuals and of society as a whole. Sociology, therefore, also describes change in social systems, and seeks to uncover the basic processes by which, under specified conditions, one state of the system leads to another, including, potentially, the state of disorganization and dissolution.

In summary, then, we may say that sociology is the study of social order, meaning thereby the underlying regularity of human social behavior. The concept of order includes the efforts to attain it and departures from it. Sociology seeks to define the units of human social action and to discover the pattern in the relation of these units—that is, to learn how they are organized as systems of action. Working with such systems of action, sociology attempts to explain their continuity through time, and to understand how and why these units and their relations change or cease to exist.

[17] Arnold Feldman and Wilbert Moore, "Industrialization and Industrialism: Convergence and Differentiation," *Transactions of the Fifth World Congress of Sociology* Vol. II (Louvain: International Sociological Association, 1962), p. 155.

three

models of society in sociological analysis

Each sociologist carries in his head one or more "models" of society and man which greatly influence what he looks for, what he sees, and what he does with his observations by way of fitting them, along with other facts, into a larger scheme of explanation. In this respect the sociologist is not different from any other scientist. Every scientist holds some general conception of the realm in which he is working, some mental picture of "how it is put together and how it works." Such models are indispensable to scientific work. It is not always possible to distinguish precisely between a scientific model and a scientific theory, and the terms are sometimes used interchangeably. A model may generate a host of theories, but one theory may be so powerful as to become, in effect, a general model. In the following discussion we use model to refer to a rather general image of the main outline of some major phenomenon, including certain leading ideas about the nature of the units involved and the pattern of their relations. A theory we take to be a heuristic device for organizing what we know, or think we know, at any particular time about some more or less explicitly posed question or issue. A theory would, therefore, be more limited and precise than a model. A theory can ordinarily be proved wrong. In the case of a model, it can usually only be judged incomplete, misleading, or unproductive.

The assumption that germs cause disease is a convenient illustration. The germ theory of disease is basically a general model, whereas the explanations of particular diseases in terms of this model may be taken as specific theories derived from the general model. Holding to this model of the cause of diseases is obviously very productive. It leads us to search for specific organisms as the cause of particular diseases, and to follow especially relevant techniques in that search. It also encourages efforts to control disease by means of procedures which kill such organisms. But holding to this model exclusively would obviously lead us astray or otherwise block our progress if we were trying to explain psychosomatic illness, dietary deficiencies, or cases of chemical poisoning. Indispensable as our models are, therefore, we pay a price for having them.

Under perfect conditions a model does not so shape our vision as to prevent us from seeing important new facts and conditions. In the best of all possible worlds, scholars would avoid too deep a personal identification with any one model, and would freely abandon their picture of the world as soon as a better one came along. In life, these ideals are seldom attained. The models with which scientists operate often become rigid; they screen and exclude from attention, or even lead to the denial of, important new facts and ideas. A scientist will often become personally identified with a particular model and resist efforts to replace it as if these were attempts to cut off that part of himself which he holds most dear. Under such circumstances the model no longer serves as a theory tentatively held, but rather becomes a fixed point of view, even a kind of scientific ideology, which limits and restricts the readiness to see things in a new light.[1] The greatest of scientists have encountered this rigidity, and some have shown it themselves.

The problem is particularly acute in sociology. Models of society and man have much more obvious, immediate, and profound moral and political implications than do most scientific conceptions. In addition, the social scientist's models are so important because very often that is all he has. The great French philosopher and scientist, Poincaré, once remarked that physicists have a subject matter, whereas sociologists engage almost exclusively in discussions of method.[2] In the natural sciences, disagreements are more readily resolved because facts must be faced according to generally accepted rules of procedure. In the social sciences, we have greater difficulty in agreeing on the facts, and not much more agreement exists about how one should go about evaluating them. The result is that social-science theories are more immune to attack, and social-science models are able to lead an absolutely charmed life. They long persist even when they give a misleading or inadequate picture of society and man. At the same time, in a realm in which the facts seem to provide such slippery footing, men are more easily led to value their models as the only firm ground on which a man can stand to view the world.

All sciences freely borrow and incorporate ideas from other fields. But it seems distinctively true of sociology that the majority of the models of society which have the widest currency have been taken over as analogies from other fields. Yet not all the models of society and man prevalent in sociology are made explicit and acknowledged by those who develop and use them. Very seldom do sociologists distinguish between a literal model, an image or conception, and a scientific theory. Not infrequently sociologists

[1] Bernard Barber, "Resistance by Scientists to Scientific Discovery" (New York: December, 1960). Paper presented before a joint annual meeting of the History of Science Society and Section, American Association for the Advancement of Science.

[2] Morris Cohen, *Reason and Nature: An Essay on the Meaning of Scientific Method* (New York: Harcourt, Brace & World, 1931), p. 350.

deny that they are in fact using the models attributed to them. When these models are made explicit, as I have made them in this chapter and the next, they inevitably emerge in a rather more bold, even stark, form which does not do full justice to the subtlety with which some of their proponents use them. Making allowances for this, we may, nevertheless, insist that most sociologists are guided by models which are relatively consistent and form a fairly clear cut orientation or even "ideology." Some of the more important models of society which underlie the work of leading sociologists, and occasionally of whole schools of sociology, are presented in the following sections of this chapter. In some cases these models appear in pairs, as opposed or polarized positions on some particular issue. It is largely in the choice of sides, in the emphasis on one or another end of some dimension, that individuals commit themselves to one or another kind of sociological work. Without some familiarity with these models, it is difficult to place many sociological studies in proper perspective. And since the models become rallying grounds for competing schools of sociology, an understanding of them is essential to identify the main intellectual currents in the field.

The Evolutionary Model

The thinking of early sociologists was dominated by a conception of man and society seen progressing up definite steps of evolution leading through ever greater complexity to some final stage of perfection. The general evolutionary model of society is represented by a large number of specific theories. Comte, for example, delineated three great stages through which all societies must go—those of conquest, defense, and industry. For each he enunciated a parallel step in the development of man's thought, which he conceived as progressing from the theological through the metaphysical to arrive ultimately at the perfection of Comte's own Positive Philosophy. While Spencer's scheme of evolution was much less grandiose, he too took the position that sociology is "the study of evolution in its most complex form."[3]

The evolutionary model treated society as if there were an imminence inherent in man's social development which requires that each stage appear in turn to play its role according to "natural law." This conception understandably tempted the promulgators of social philosophies to capture the evolutionary theory and to use it in support of their political positions. The American sociologist William Graham Sumner, for example, justified the privileges of the advantaged classes over the disadvantaged on the grounds that such differentiation was a law of nature in keeping with the principle of the survival of the fittest. Sumner, who has been labeled a "Social Darwinist," used the idea of evolution, as had Spencer, to block efforts at reform and social change, arguing that social evolution must follow its own course, dictated by nature. "That is why," he said, "it is the greatest folly of which a man can be capable, to sit down with a slate and pencil to plan out a new social world."[4]

The evolutionary approach to societal development was also used to support the arguments of the extreme left in politics. Marx and Engels were greatly influenced by the work of the anthropologist L. H. Morgan, who sought to prove that all societies went through fixed stages of development,

[3] Herbert Spencer, *The Study of Sociology* (New York: D. Appleton, 1873), p. 350.

[4] William Graham Sumner, "The Absurd Effort to Make the World Over," in A. G. Keller and M. R. Davis (eds.), *Essays of William Graham Sumner* (New Haven: Yale University Press, 1934), p. 106.

each succeeding the other, from savagery through barbarism to civilization. Marx and Engels maintained that each stage of civilization, such as feudalism, prepared the ground for the next. It contained within itself "the seeds of its own destruction," and would inevitably be succeeded by that stage next "higher" on the scale of evolution. On this basis they argued that the "stage" of capitalism had so far advanced the rationalization of production and its concentration in large units as to make socialism and planning historically necessary and inevitable. They also added the idea that each era resisted the birth of the new, and concluded that the next step in social evolution could be attained only by violent revolution.

Common to both Comte's and Marx' theories is the assumption that each society does, indeed must, pass through a fixed and limited number of stages in a given sequence. For that reason they are referred to as *unilinear theories* of evolution. Such theories long dominated the sociological imagination. In each generation the leading sociologist could be expected, each in his turn, to come forward with a new scheme for classifying the stages of social development. Since these later schemes were generally less sweeping and less explicitly labeled, they should perhaps be called *quasi-evolutionary theories.*

For Durkheim the most important dimension of society was the degree of specialization within it, or as he called it, "the division of labor." He believed there was an historical trend, or evolution, from a low to a high degree of specialization, and that important consequences followed from this. Durkheim distinguished two main types of society on the basis of how far the division of labor had progressed. The first depended on what he called "mechanical solidarity." It was typified by the smaller community in which the degree of specialization was limited, and people were held together by tight bonds through their immersion in strong primary institutions such as the extended family and the local religion. The second type of society was based on what he called "organic solidarity." In this system relations are less intimate and personal, and people are tied to one another mainly by common interests, by contract, and by more abstract symbols. Durkheim believed that this second type always evolved from and succeeded the first as the degree of specialization, the divisions of labor, increased.[5]

Some years before Durkheim published *The Division of Labor*, a comparable model, assuming the same direction of development, was presented by the German sociologist Ferdinand Tönnies, who distinguished community-like *gemeinschaft* and corporate (*gesellschaft*) types of society. The first corresponded quite well to Durkheim's mechanical solidarity, the second to his organic type. Numerous others put forth similar ideas. The scheme most recently to win attention was developed by the American anthropologist Robert Redfield, who elaborated on the contrast between "folk" and "urban" society.[6] The regular rediscovery, restatement, and reiteration of the same basic dichotomy of social types suggests that the distinction being made is very fundamental. It also illustrates the difficulty sociology has in getting beyond the stage of developing models of society, and moving on to the point where it can convincingly put them to work in explaining major social processes.

Cyclical theories are an important variant on the unilinear conceptions

[5] Émile Durkheim (G. Simpson, trans.), *The Division of Labor in Society* (Glencoe, Ill.: The Free Press, 1933).

[6] Robert Redfield, "The Folk Society," *American Journal of Sociology* (1947), Vol. LII, No. 4.

of evolution. Such theories set out a certain number of stages or cycles which any long-enduring culture may go through more than once, even repeatedly. Pareto's theory of the "circulation of elites" is essentially of this variety.[7]

Among the more recent examples of this perspective is Professor Sorokin's theory of social and cultural dynamics. He sees societies as passing through three stages, each dominated by a system of truth. In the *ideational* phase truth is revealed by the grace of God and is based on *faith; sensate* culture is dominated by the testimony of our *senses;* and in *idealistic* culture there is a synthesis of both, dominated by *reason.*[8] Professor Sorokin places contemporary European and American culture in the last stages of the disintegration of sensate culture, and argues that the only way out of our "crisis" is a new synthesis of faith and sensation. "Such," he says, "was the invariable course of the the great crises of the past. Such is the way out of our own crisis. There is no other possibility." [9]

The *universal theory* of evolution [10] grants that *every* society does not necessarily go through the same fixed stages of development. It argues, rather, that the culture of *mankind,* taken as a whole, has followed a definite line of evolution. Principles of this type are found clearly enunciated in the work of Spencer, as when he said that mankind had progressed from small groups to large and from simple to compound and doubly compound, or, in more general terms, from the homogeneous to the heterogeneous.[11] The anthropologist Leslie White has been a leading exponent of this conception.[12]

Professor White held that technology, particularly the amount of energy harnessed and the way in which it is used, determines the forms and content of culture and society. The evolution of culture has not been even, he argued, but proceeds in great spurts as new sources of energy are harnessed. Thus the agricultural revolution on which the great civilizations of the Old World were built was followed by a relatively long period of stagnation until the Fuel Age was introduced in the New World about 1800. Although this theory holds that there is a clear line of advance for the human species as a whole, it does not argue that each society necessarily goes through all or most of the stages of development. On the contrary, "all share in the progress of each" as a result of the *diffusion* of technological advances. Furthermore, with each leap forward the rate of development is accelerated, in the sense that population and energy per capita increase at an increasing rate. In one important respect, however, White shares the orientation of the older evolutionists—he sees the whole development focusing on a single distant point toward which we are "inexorably" moving. The future promises for all mankind "higher levels of integration . . . greater concentrations of political power and control . . . a single political organization that will embrace the entire planet and the whole human race." [13]

Similar ideas were greatly elaborated by William Ogburn, who stressed the role of invention in social change, dealt with the acceleration in the rate

[7] See also Chap. 5.

[8] Pitirim A. Sorokin, *Social and Cultural Dynamics,* one-volume ed. (Boston: Sargent, 1957).

[9] Pitirim A. Sorokin, *The Crisis of Our Age* (New York: Dutton, 1941), p. 324.

[10] I here follow the terminology suggested in Julian Steward, "Evolution and Process," in A. Kroeber (ed.), *Anthropology Today* (Chicago: University of Chicago Press, 1953), pp. 313–326.

[11] Herbert Spencer, *Principles of Sociology,* 3rd ed. Vol. I (New York: D. Appleton, 1910), p. 471.

[12] Leslie White, *The Science of Culture* (New York: Farrar, Strauss, 1949).

[13] *Ibid.,* pp. 338 *ff.*

of growth in material culture, and gave birth to the famous law of "culture lag"—which stated that changes in our non-material culture—i.e., in our ideas and social arrangements—always lag behind changes in material culture —i.e., in our technology and inventions.[14]

Still another type of evolutionary theory, which we may call the *multilinear,*[15] has more recently emerged. Those who share this perspective attempt to explain neither the straight-line evolution of each society, nor the progress of mankind as a whole, but rather concentrate on much more limited sequences of development. They might ask, for example: "In all cases in which there has been a shift from hunting to agriculture in the economic realm, has there also been a particular corresponding change in the family system?" This type of question is interesting and important, but it does not bear much resemblance to more "traditional" evolutionary thinking.

Recently some of the younger sociologists, particularly in the United States, have become interested in the implications of the ever wider diffusion of industrialism. In the tradition of White and Ogburn, they have closely examined the culture and social structure of countries all over the world to assess the extent to which the widspread adoption of industrial forms of production encouraged the development of uniform institutions and social patterns. Arnold Rose expressed a view, ever more widely held, when he said in his introduction to *The Institutions of Advanced Societies:* "A world culture affecting all advanced societies has been developing for the past four centuries or so . . . . The source and heart of this common culture lies in world trade and industrialization and their immediate consequences in urbanization, specialization, secularization, and the opening of possibilities for social mobility, universal education, and improvement in the material standard of living." [16]

This latest school of sociology does not really use an evolutionary model, universal, or multilinear, but rather holds a conception of society which assumes that changes in any part of the social system will have important consequences for other parts and for the system as a whole. That model, often called the organismic, or structural-functional, will be discussed in the next section.

A mass of evidence has been accumulated to show that societies do not pass through unilinear stages. In addition, the condition of the world during the twentieth century has made it difficult to believe either that contemporary society represents the highest stage of man's development or that he will inevitably move forward to develop still higher—i.e., superior—forms of social life. Consequently the unilinear evolutionary model of social development has very little interest for most contemporary sociologists. The universal theory of evolution also fails to capture their attention as an important theme. They seem content to leave the continuing study of unilinear and universal evolution to anthropologists. Much of what the multilinear theory offers, they feel, they can better understand through the use of other models. The evolutionary model of social development in all its aspects has, therefore, largely been abandoned by sociologists.

[14] William F. Ogburn, *Social Change with Respect to Culture and Original Nature* (New York: Viking, 1950).

[15] Julian Steward, "Evolution and Progress," in A. Kroeber (ed.), *Anthropology Today,* pp. 313–326.

[16] Arnold Rose (ed.), *The Institutions of Advanced Societies* (Minneapolis: University of Minnesota Press, 1958), p. 26. See also Alex Inkeles, "Industrial Man: The Relation of Status to Experience, Perception and Value," *American Journal of Sociology* (1960), LXVI:1–31.

With the rejection of the evolutionary view, some of the activities which it stimulated have also been slighted. The evolutionary perspective required a strong commitment to the study of history, especially man's early history. That interest has largely died out in modern sociology. The effective application of an evolutionary scheme rested on developing typologies of society. Contemporary sociologists generally look on this as rather an empty game—a kind of playing with boxes. One consequence of their neglect of history has been that sociologists played only a minor role in shaping the study of new forms of society, such as the totalitarian systems of Europe and the "new nations" emerging from tribal and colonial conditions in Asia and Africa.[17] The growing interest of younger sociologists in the consequences of industrialism and in the resultant forms of industrial society may, however, be the path by which some types of work earlier fostered by the evolutionary perspective may be restored to a place of importance in contemporary sociology.

The Organismic Model: Structural-Functionalism

Analogies between society and living organisms are as old as social thought. Plato spoke of the three different elements of society as the thinking, or rational; the feeling, or spirited; and the appetitive parts, each represented by a particular social class. The organic analogy was widely prevalent in pre-Comteian thought, and it is not surprising that it appeared very early in sociology's history. The most important manifestation of this pattern has been in the linked concepts of "structure" and "function," which already appear in Spencer, were used by Durkheim, and figured prominently in the work of the great sociologically oriented British anthropologists, Malinowski and Radcliffe-Brown.[18] Through these and other channels this perspective came to have substantial influence in American sociology, particularly among students and followers of Talcott Parsons, and it is now generally known as the structural-functional school of sociology.

There are, of course, variations among structural-functionalists in emphasis, and in the completeness of their devotion to an organismic analogy of society.[19] The basic perspective of the structural-functional point of view emerges in its prime emphasis on society, and on the interrelations of its institutions, rather than on the individual or groups such as the family. The main question to which it addresses itself is this: "How is social life

[17] For important exceptions see: Barrington Moore, Jr., *Soviet Politics: The Dilemma of Power* (Cambridge: Harvard University Press, 1950); Raymond Bauer, Alex Inkeles, and Clyde Kluckhohn, *How the Soviet System Works* (Cambridge: Harvard University Press, 1959); Daniel Lerner, *The Passing of Traditional Society: Modernizing the Middle East* (Glencoe, Ill.: The Free Press, 1958); Monroe Berger, *The Arab World Today* (London: Nicolson, 1962); Wilbert Moore and Arnold Feldman, *Labor Commitment and Social Change in Developing Areas* (New York: Social Science Research Council, 1960); Marion Levy, *Family Revolution in Modern China* (Cambridge: Harvard University Press, 1949).

[18] Herbert Spencer, *Principles of Sociology;* Émile Durkheim (J. W. Swain, trans.), *Elementary Forms of Religious Life* (New York: Macmillan, 1926); Bronislaw Malinowski, *Crime and Custom in Savage Society* (London: Trench and Trubner, 1926); A. R. Radcliffe-Brown, *Structure and Function in Primitive Society* (Glencoe, Ill.: The Free Press, 1952).

[19] For a general view of the structural-functional position the following sources are indispensable: Robert K. Merton, *Social Theory and Social Structure* (Glencoe, Ill.: The Free Press, 1957); Kingsley Davis, *Human Society* (New York: Macmillan, 1949); Marion Levy, *The Structure of Society* (Princeton: Princeton University Press, 1952); Talcott Parsons, *The Structure of Social Action* (Glencoe, Ill.: The Free Press, 1949), and *The Social System* (Glencoe, Ill.: The Free Press, 1951).

maintained and carried forward in time despite the complete turnover in the membership of society with every new generation?" The basic answer it gives is: "Social life persists because societies find means (structures) whereby they fulfill the needs (functions) which are either pre-conditions or consequences of organized social life."

The evolutionary and functional views are not opposed to each other, but their interests and emphases are different. The evolutionary perspective is similar to Comte's idea of "social dynamics," whereas the structural-functional approach is a contemporary relative of his "social statics." The evolutionist is concerned with the classification of societies according to an established evolutionary scale. Time, stages of development, and change are, therefore, central to his interest. The structural-functional approach involves a more limited time perspective. It stops the motions of the system at a fixed point in time, it order to understand how, at that moment, it works as a system. When considering a particular institution, those guided by the evolutionary perspective try to understand how the evolutionary stage of the society as a whole shapes the form of the institution. The structural-functionalists will emphasize more how the institution contributed to keeping the society in operation. It is readily apparent that this approach could easily lead the functionalist to neglect the process of change—a point to which we will return shortly.

The objective of the adherents of the structural-functional view is to delineate the conditions and demands of social life, and to trace the process whereby a given society arranges to meet its needs. To choose an obvious example, if a society is to continue, it must periodically find new members. In all known societies the need is met by some form of family system. The family is the institution which acts "for" society to ensure fulfillment of the functions of sexual reproduction, of early care of the dependent infant, and of his initial training in the ways of the society in which he will live.

The structural-functional analyst must also deal with the way in which the different structures are co-ordinated and integrated to preserve the unity of society as a complete system (or organism). This idea was already quite clearly articulated by Comte when he said "sociology consists in the investigation of the laws of action and reaction of the different parts of the social system." [20]

The structural-functional point of view has undoubtedly contributed significantly to the development of sociological thought and research. Many features of society which otherwise are puzzling and seem to have no reason for existence become comprehensible when seen in relation to their "function" (i.e., their contribution to the flow of social life). Thus, from a functionalist point of view, rather violent, and even individually harmful *rites de passage* may be treated as useful training in the sort of publicly sanctioned bravery and endurance which is required in a society which relies on hunting scarce or dangerous game as its chief source of food. Or the romantic love complex in our own society may be seen as serving the function of providing the "push" required to free young people from the dependence encouraged by our family system, thus getting them to accept the responsibilities of marriage.

This perspective has also made us sensitive to many functions important to the continuance of social life which we otherwise neglect or to which we assign insufficient importance. Durkheim and his associates did much to clarify the significance of public ceremonials as a way of increasing social

[20] Auguste Comte (H. Martineau, trans.), *The Positive Philosophy of Auguste Comte* (New York: Blanchard, 1855), p. 457.

solidarity,[21] and the studies by his disciple Marcel Mauss on *The Gift* [22] revealed in detail how seemingly unimportant elements of social life can in fact serve important functions in preserving the bonds which tie one individual and one group to another, thereby preserving the unity of society as a whole.

Sensitivity to the interrelations of the component elements of a social system has increased our understanding of social change. Our awareness that changes in one part of society have important implications for other parts of the system has broadened our perspective, enabling us better to understand why so often innovations are so slowly adopted (we usually say "resisted"), and why changes introduced to effect one particular purpose so often have consequences quite different from those initially intended and anticipated.

The structural-functional point of view has also been a great boon to comparative studies, especially those involving primitive cultures and others very strange or foreign to us. Many societies seem to have no government and no economic institutions as we understand them. The functional emphasis sensitizes us to search for the less obvious ways in which these societies arrange to provide for the flow of goods and services or to control the legitimate use of force. We are thus enabled to broaden our horizons concerning the possibilities for variation in the forms of social life, and are, as well, made aware of the practical limits to utopian schemes of social organization.

The dangers and difficulties inherent in this point of view are not difficult to discern. The criticism most often cited is that the structural-functional approach is teleological. Function seems only another word for purpose, and it is often argued that a person can have purpose but that a collectivity cannot. One can certainly sensibly reply that many groups act so effectively in unison that it seems "as if" they were a single organism possessed of only a single will or purpose. In addition, some of the leading exponents of the structural-functional point of view use "function" only to mean "as a consequence of," thus avoiding the question of value or purpose.

But even using function in this more limited sense does not avoid the most serious complaint directed against the structural-functionalists, which is that they often fail to specify for whom or what something is "functional." What is functional for the society may not be functional for the individual—say slavery in ancient Greece or on the cotton-growing plantations of the southern United States before 1840. The functionalist point of view easily leads one to underemphasize the importance of the individual and his needs relative to those of the group. The focus of a man's research, and the problems and materials he emphasizes, will obviously be different if he assumes that society was brought into existence and acts mainly to serve the needs of the individual rather than believing that society is nature's prime interest and that the individual exists mainly to serve the needs of society.

What is functional for one individual or group may not be functional for another. To say that we can resolve this ambiguity by choosing that alternative which is more functional for the society is not an adequate answer unless we can get agreement on exactly what constitutes our "society" and what is or is not functional for it. Unfortunately we cannot always agree on who, or what, is meant by the term "the society." The Greek slaves were not considered members of ancient Greek society, although in some regions they were the majority of the residents. Even if social scientists can agree on

[21] Durkheim, *Elementary Forms of Religious Life*.

[22] Marcel Mauss (I. Cunnison, trans.), *The Gift* (Glencoe, Ill.: The Free Press, 1954).

who are the members of a given society, they may find that the members themselves do not agree on what is in society's interest. And even if the people agree, they may nevertheless be directing their society along the road to ruin and dissolution, which is hardly functional from any point of view.

The structural-functional approach encourages a search for the function of every existing structure. The imagination is generally not lacking to devise such functions. Consequently, everything which exists in a society at any given time is easily assumed to be there because it is "functional." Presumably, if it were not there, some need of society would be left more or less unfulfilled. This principle can obviously be used to justify opposition to experimentation and social change, on the grounds that what exists, being functional, cannot be removed without dire repercussions ensuing.

Despite these defects and dangers in the model, every sociologist to a degree is something of a structural-functional analyst. There are very few sociologists who would argue that there is no order or system in social life. Not many would hold that society can properly be conceived only as a great buzzing blooming confusion, or that the patterns which the sociologist purports to see in social life are nothing more than illusions. It is doubtful that any sociologist would deny that the continuation of social life requires that certain functions, such as the socialization of children, the control of violence, and the regulation of sex be performed by some social agency, or would propose that it is unimportant to know which does the job and how. Nor would many challenge the importance of studying the distinctive structures of society to see what functions they perform.

Considering its potential universal appeal, it is interesting that the structural-functional approach is the object of such regular and intense criticism. In part this criticism rests on the difficulties cited above—such as the tendency to invent functions for everything in sight. In part it rests on the tendency of those who emphasize structural-functional analysis to act as if they have *the* master key to sociology. Perhaps the greatest challenge to this point of view, however, comes from those who prefer what they call a "conflict model" of society. They place "conflict" in opposition to "equilibrium," which, in their opinion, is the most important concept for those sharing the structural-functional approach.

Equilibrium vs. Conflict Models

The equilibrium model of society is a special version of the functionalist approach. Its critics claim that it deflects attention from the facts of social tension and conflict, and therefore serves as a politically conservative influence in sociological thinking. Conservatism is not a condition inherent in the structural-functional perspective, which is quite well able to handle most problems of change. Indeed, the theory explicitly states that prolonged failure to meet certain functions will bring a dissolution of society, that a change in structure will influence ability to perform function, and that a change in one sub-structure will generally affect other sub-structures in the same system. In the special case of the equilibrium model, however, the problem of change does tend to drop out of sight in favor of concentration on the "steady state" of the system. This defect is not an inescapable characteristic of the equilibrium model, but in practice it tends to develop rather consistently.

The equilibrium theory has been most fully elaborated by Talcott Parsons and some of his students. The general model for this theory, one explicitly acknowledged as such by its exponents, is the concept of homeostasis as applied to human physiology by Walter B. Cannon in his widely read book *The Wisdom of the Body*. Typical of Cannon's mode of analysis is his discussion of the processes which insure that the tissues are steadily supplied with blood, thus serving to bring them nutriment and to carry off waste. Cannon showed how, following any lesion, the body immediately brings into play a series of mechanisms, such as contraction of the blood vessels leading to the point of injury, a series of adjustments which insure clotting, increased production of red blood cells, and the like. The body in this way prevents blood loss from too drastically upsetting its balance, and then gradually sets about restoring the system to its former equilibrium.[23]

Following this model, Parsons and others have conceived of society as also attempting by more or less automatic adjustments to redress the balance of its equilibrium when it is upset by internal or external forces. To give an example, let us assume that in some strata of society the family is weak and children are often abandoned and generally not properly socialized. If the values of the society stressed the importance of reasonable care and opportunity for all young people, the situation would represent a source of strain on the value system. If, in addition, the affected areas produced a disproportionately large number of juvenile deliquents, a social nuisance would have been created. Taken together these conditions would be elements of disequilibrium in the social system. The equilibrium model would suggest that a society faced with this situation could be expected to take certain corrective measures. These might include intensified social work with the families to strengthen them and to teach new ways of child-rearing, the development of community centers to work with the youth, and investments in new housing to eliminate blighted areas. With intelligent and timely effort on a sufficient scale, the original source of "infection" would presumably be brought under control. In time the affected group would, hopefully, be led to adopt new habits in the care of children and in its relations to society. The latter would, then, have had its equilibrium restored.

As a special case of structural-functional analysis, the equilibrium model has some of the virtues of the former. But the analogy suggested by Cannon's studies does not bring anything important to what structural-functional analysis already contained, and the newly added defects are fairly obvious. There is no end of historical evidence that societies regularly fail to control what happens to them; they change radically and very often simply die out. Second, to apply the analogy of physiological homeostasis, we must know just what is the optimal state of the system to which it should return when disturbed. This may be clear with regard to human temperature, but it is not nearly so obvious with regard to social climate. Third, we need to know what brings the process about. In Cannon's model the necessary adjustments are clearly built into the cell structure, the organs, and the body chemistry of the human organism, but we cannot, with equal preciseness, point out the specific "guardians of equilibrium" in society.

The sharpest criticism of the equilibrium model is launched by those who oppose to it what they call a conflict model of society. It is an illusion, they say, to believe that society, especially modern society, is in some sort of harmonious balance to the preservation of which everyone and everything is devoted. The critics of the equilibrium theory argue that far from being in a state of harmonious balance, most societies are usually experiencing conflict, particularly a conflict of interests. In other words, they maintain that

[23] Walter B. Cannon, *The Wisdom of the Body* (New York: Norton, 1932).

rather than consensus, the basic condition of social life is dissension, arising through the competition for power and advantage between the different groups. The dominant social process, therefore, is not the steady effort to restore harmony or equilibrium, but the endless struggle between those without advantages, who wish to secure them, and those with privileges who wish either to get more or to prevent others from taking what is available. The equilibrium model, say the proponents of the conflict theory, consciously or unwittingly, becomes a support for the status quo. Instead of being a lens which sharpens our perspective and puts social reality in focus, it becomes a pair of rose-colored glasses which distort reality, screening out the harsh facts about conflict of purpose and interest in human affairs.

The conflict model of society has recently been most extensively and vigorously advanced by Lewis Coser, Ralf Dahrendorf, and Johan Galtung,[24] but it finds strong support in a number of other critiques of modern sociology, such as that by C. Wright Mills. There is certainly some justice in their criticism. An analysis of current sociological writing will reveal much less description of community and class conflict than the facts would warrant.

To say this is not to declare the conflict model more correct than the equilibrium model. We are unfortunately not in a position to say which model is more nearly "the right one." Indeed, when the question is put in such general form, it is probably unanswerable. Societies display both conflict and tendencies toward consensus. Periods of relative stability may alternate with periods of intense conflict and rapid change. Different societies in different times and places display more of one than the other. To say this is to utter more than a platitude, yet this is a truth that does not carry us very far. What is most important for us to recognize at this point in our inquiry into sociological analysis is that sociologists select and emphasize different facts depending upon the model of society they favor.

The philosopher of science, Morris Cohen, has pointed out that social science typically operates with sets of opposed generalizations, within which both of the generalizations are to some extent true. He cites as an example the idea that people are moved by a social instinct, and the opposed notion that they are inherently individualistic and even anti-social. Some day we may be able to give precise weight to each such factor, and then, in given situations, to balance one against the other. In limited degree this is already happening in contemporary sociology. Until we make further progress along this line, we should be responsive to Cohen's dictum that "science means the rigorous weighing of all the evidence, including a full consideration of all possible theories (which is the true antidote for bias or prejudice)." [25]

The Physical Science Model

One of the oldest models of society is provided by the physical world. Indeed before he coined the term sociology Comte referred to the new field as "social physics." The idea reappeared regularly in the course of sociological development, and to this day has substantial influence on the thinking of many sociologists. Even so consistently a partisan of the structural-functional point of view as Talcott Parsons from time to time formulates

[24] Lewis Coser, *The Functions of Social Conflict* (Glencoe, Ill.: The Free Press, 1956); Ralf Dahrendorf, *Class and Class Conflict in Industrial Society* (Stanford: Stanford University Press, 1959); Johan Galtung, "Pacifism from a Sociological Point of View," *Journal of Social Issues* (1959), 3:67–84.

[25] Cohen, *Reason and Nature: An Essay on the Meaning of Scientific Method*, p. 347.

a sociological principle obviously modeled after a typical law of physics. His principle of inertia, for example, states: "A given process of [social] action will continue unchanged in rate and direction unless impeded or deflected by opposing motivational forces." [26]

Several sociologists, notably George Lundberg and Stuart Dodd,[27] have become deeply identified with the position that sociology must follow the pattern of the natural sciences. Indeed they often take phenomena from the physical world as explicit models for social events, and suggest that laws applicable to the former can explain the latter. Contemporary social physics has gone so far as to assert that the laws which explain the flight of a piece of paper before the wind may also explain the movements of a man fleeing from a mob. The intensity of the argument aroused by this idea is typical of the profound gulf which separates those influenced by a physical model of society and those who most vigorously challenge its adequacy. The gulf widens when the principles of physics used are taken from the field of mechanics.

The most obvious, and most often cited, explanation for the appeal of the physical science model is that the success of physicists and chemists has given their approach an aura of power and prestige so great that people are inevitably attracted to it. Some sociologists do believe that physical science has the magic key which unlocks all doors, even when there seems little surface validity in the analogy between physical and social phenomena. The precision of expression which characterizes physical science, with its dimensions of space and time, its forces and vectors, greatly tempts those who weary of the ambiguity of so many sociological terms, the vagueness of the relations specified between variables, and the indefiniteness of the conclusions reached.

We should be careful to distinguish between the general procedures of science and particular theories of the physical and chemical sciences. Sociology clearly shares in and benefits from the general advances in scientific method, to which the physical scientists have contributed so greatly. Useful as the general principles of science may be, however, it does not follow that particular physical science principles, such as those governing the attraction of bodies in the law of gravitation, must be illuminating models for explaining social phenomena. The direct application of explanatory models drawn from physics and chemistry has done very little to advance sociological analysis. Sociological formulas couched in the language of physics are as a rule quite empty, because we are unable to specify the units of such terms as "rate of change" or "direction." The development of formulas such as the Parsons' principle of inertia, therefore, tends to be little more than an exercise.

Even if we can give meaningful content to the concepts drawn from physics, there is no reason to assume that the relations between the analogous elements in the social realm will be the same as in the physical world. Indeed, there is every reason to doubt that they will. Therefore, no particular benefit is gained by the laborious process of translating sociological problems into the language of physics or chemistry.

The difficulty of such translation can be well illustrated by the history of efforts to explain "the observed movement of population in space." This certainly sounds like the sort of problem to which a physical model would

[26] Talcott Parsons, Robert F. Bales, and Edward Shils, *Working Papers in the Theory of Action* (Glencoe, Ill.: The Free Press, 1953), p. 102.

[27] See George Lundberg, *Foundations of Sociology* (New York: Macmillan, 1939); and Stuart Dodd, *Dimensions of Society* (New York: Macmillan, 1942).

be relevant. George K. Zipf of Harvard, a philologist and leading exponent of the social physics approach, sought to explain such movement by what he called the "principle of least effort," which he regarded as a natural law. He gave this principle many applications, using it to explain some features of language as well as the movement of population. According to the principle of least effort, the number of people going from one city to another should be a function of the distance separating them, since the effort required to cover greater distances would presumably increase as did the distance. His formula [28] was none too successful in describing the actual flow of population, at least so far as migration from one city to another was concerned.

Further analysis of the problem by Samuel Stouffer showed how we could predict the observed population movements much better by introducing the idea of "intervening opportunities." Stouffer reasoned that the chance that people moving from a given city would settle in some other distant city should be influenced by the opportunities along the way which might initially attract the migrant and then keep him from going on. Stouffer gave very precise expression to this idea [29] and he and others firmly demonstrated the factual superiority of their theory over that originally presented by Zipf. In later studies Stouffer further modified the theory to take account of the influence which other migrants competing for the same scarce opportunities might have on the movement of people from one city to another.[30] This adjustment still further improved his ability to account for the facts of intercity migration. In his last paper on the subject, published shortly before his death, he urged those who would work on the problem in the future to abandon the measurement of distance merely in terms of miles and to use instead some more *social* measure such as transportation costs.

The precise details of this study are not important to us at this point. What is relevant is the failure of a simple physical formula to account satisfactorily for a social phenomenon to which it seemed maximally applicable. The principle of least effort involves no sociological concepts—it deals with social phenomena entirely in terms of physical units—number of persons, distance, and the like. And it fails adequately to account for the facts on the migration of people from one city to another. Improved explanation of such movement was possible only when Stouffer and others introduced concepts such as "intervening opportunities," "competing migrants," and "economic costs," terms which have no exact analogue in the physical world. The explanatory principle finally elaborated by Stouffer, therefore, bears very little relation to the original developed by Zipf. Zipf's theory did lead him to select an interesting social problem, but his physical science model kept him from developing a satisfactory explanation of it.

Doubts about the relevance for social science of models developed initially to deal with physical and chemical phenomena should not be allowed

[28] George K. Zipf, "The $P_1 \cdot P_2/D$ Hypothesis on the Intercity Movement of Persons," *American Sociological Review* (1946), XI:677. The exact formulation was as follows: "The number of persons that move between any two communities in the United States whose respective populations are P_1 and P_2, and which are separated by the shortest transportation distance, D, will be proportionate to the ratio $P_1 \cdot P_2/D$ subject to the effect of modifying factors."

[29] Samuel Stouffer, "Intervening Opportunities: A Theory Relating Mobility and Distance," *American Sociological Review* (1940), VI:845–867.

[30] Samuel Stouffer, "Intervening Opportunities and Competing Migrants," *Journal of Regional Studies* (1960), II:1–26. His theory stated specifically that "the number of people going 'S' distance from a point is directly proportional to the number of opportunities on the perimeter of a circle within radius 'S' and inversely proportional to the number of opportunities on or within that circle."

to obscure the more general issue whether sociology is or can be a science. When we show that one or another model from physics or chemistry fits social facts very poorly, if at all, we do not thereby settle the question whether there can be a science of social phenomena. The tendency to assume we have settled the issue gains force from the fact that some of these who most vigorously press for the use of natural science *methods* in sociology are also these who slip most easily into using physical laws as models for sociological analysis. The two, however, are quite distinct. Concepts borrowed from physics probably have the least relevance for sociology, and, in fact, are usually a trap. The distinctive methods of physics and chemistry are also unlikely to ever be important for social science. The physical sciences can, however, offer the social sciences stimulation by suggesting some very general explanatory approaches or models, providing they are not applied too literally. And the general procedures of science certainly have relevance for sociology.[31]

Statistical and Mathematical Models

Most sociologists who use statistical methods of analysis think of them as tools or techniques. Many, perhaps the majority, would be somewhat surprised if you were to point out that in the mere adoption of a particular statistical technique they are accepting a certain mathematical model as an appropriate description of at least some aspect of the social world. Sociologists tend to think of their techniques as "neutral" and as not implicitly committing them to any particular view of the world. In fact, no statistical technique can be intelligently applied unless certain assumptions are made or conditions met. In meeting them, the sociologist is accepting certain mathematical relations as a model, even if tentative, of the social relations he is studying. Since the statistics used by sociologists tend to follow the theory of probability, sociologists using it are in effect adopting a probabilistic model of society.

After World War II the application of mathematical models to social phenomena became an increasingly popular and explicit procedure. The application of such models generally follows one of two paths. A research worker observes that his results seem again and again to follow a given form. He may then look around to discover if there is some mathematical model which seems to fit this pattern, and, by direct test, will apply it to his data. If it fits closely, he is likely to use the mathematical model as a basis for predicting subsequent observations of the same phenomenon. The model may also suggest to him types of data, or may even predict relationships, with which he has not yet dealt.

Robert Bales' study of interaction in small groups provides an example.[32] In his small discussion groups Professor Bales recorded and counted each action directed by and to any person. He then ranked each participant in the group according to how many acts were directed toward him by others. In some of his groups Bales observed that about 45 per cent of all the acts that occurred were directed toward the man who ranked first. About 18 per cent of all acts were directed toward the man who stood second, and about 6 per cent were directed toward the man who received least attention, say in a 6-man group. Since this looked rather like the pattern one obtains with harmonic curves, Professor Bales sought to apply this mathematical

[31] This is a theme to which we will return when we discuss the possibility of a science of man in Chap. 7.

[32] Other illustrations of Bales' technique are given in Chap. 7.

model to the interaction in groups varying in size from 3 to 8 men. He reached a striking conclusion that whatever the size of the group, up to 8 men, basically the same pattern was present. The man who received most attention was the object of about 45 per cent of all action in the group; the second was the object of about 18 per cent; and the rest divided the remainder systematically according to the size of the group. The harmonic curve, it developed, provided an approximate, although far from perfect, fit as a model for the observed pattern.[33]

The procedure is not always so simple. The data available to a sociologist may not so clearly suggest the relevance of a particular kind of mathematics. Indeed, it is often necessary to construct new mathematical models in order to deal with the pattern of relations present in a given realm.

The work of Herbert A. Simon, contained in his book *Models of Man: Social and Rational*,[34] represents one of the most successful and impressive applications of mathematical models to social science problems. He has suggested how set theory[35] may be useful in describing political power or authority, how differential equations may be used to translate into mathematics the propositions developed by Professor George Homans to describe interaction in small groups, and how a stochastic process[36] model can serve to describe a series of puzzling statistical regularities which are common to the distribution of city sizes, incomes, word frequencies, and frequencies of publication. This last problem suggested that the mathematics of stochastic processes may provide a general model for describing widespread phenomena of "social imitation."

Like any other conception of the social world, mathematical models affect the work of sociologists. They divert his attention to problems to which mathematics seems most relevant, and away from those which do not lend themselves to such treatment. Since it is usually difficult to transform or "translate" actual observations into the terms used in the model, an interest in mathematical models encourages either intensive preöccupation with problems of measurement, or a happy game in which the analyst abandons any pretense that his model is applicable to the real world, and simply concerns himself with the "as if" world described by his model.

If we acknowledge that to work with statistical procedure is in fact to adopt a mathematical model, in this case a probabilistic one, then we must admit that mathematical models have already had a tremendous effect on sociology. Indeed, they have transformed it. If we regard statistics as merely a neutral technique, then we should conclude that so far the explicit use of mathematical models in sociology has made only a very limited contribution. In the future, of course, such models may well give very impressive results, but only if we heed Professor Simon's double caution:

> First . . . we do well to avoid *a priori* philosophical commitments to models of particular kinds—whether they be probabilistic or deterministic, continuous or discrete, analytic or set-theoretic. . . .

[33] Robert F. Bales, *Interaction Process Analysis* (Cambridge: Addison-Wesley, 1951).

[34] Herbert A. Simon, *Models of Man: Social and Rational* (New York: Wiley, 1957).

[35] *Set theory* is a mathematics developed to deal with sets or classes of things rather than numbers. In the social sciences it has been the basis of game theory, formulated to calculate the "return" and "loss" involved in particular decisions.

[36] In a general sense, a stochastic process connotes any statistical process. More specifically, it is any statistical process involving sequences of events in which the probability of an event depends on the preceding events. Language, learning, population movements, and chain reactions have all been studied with stochastic processes.

> Second, we must not expect to find the models we need ready-made in a mathematical textbook. If we are lucky, we shall not have to invent new mathematics, but we are likely to have to assemble our model from a variety of new materials. For this reason we should be wary of borrowing, in any wholesale fashion, analogical models from the natural sciences. Analogies there will undoubtedly be . . . but it will be safer to notice them after we have developed our theories than to attempt to employ them as a basis of theory construction.[37]

Professor Simon's strictures may themselves be taken as a model of the sound judgment one needs to exercise when choosing social science models.

Models, Propositions, and Truth

Even within sociology the models of society are numerous and diverse. Naturally, the question arises: Which are correct, which true, which false? The question cannot be answered. Indeed, the question itself must be rejected. All are correct, in part. Each holds a piece of the truth. No one is more nearly the absolute truth, because there is no absolute truth. To ask which is truer is to fail to understand the proper function of such models. They are devices for focusing our attention. They point to problems; they suggest relevant data; they imply appropriate techniques by which the data may be collected and methods by which they may be analyzed. A particular proposition or hypothesis may be true or false. Sometimes, of course, a model is specific enough to constitute a precise hypothesis. The unilinear theory of evolution was of that type. Most models, however, provide more general perspectives. Such models can only be useful or useless, stimulating or uninteresting, fruitful or sterile, but not true or false.

To say this may seem to be admitting that sociology is not, and never can be, a science. That depends, of course, on one's conception of science. Many people have an image of science as much more orderly, precise, and unified than it actually is. What any science knows is ordinarily summed up in a set of theories which are only partially integrated and are sometimes quite divorced one from the other. Alfred North Whitehead notes in *Science and the Modern World* that Huyghen's wave theory of light, although it opened great vistas, failed to account for the shadows cast by obstructing objects. This the corpuscular theory of light, favored by Newton, did quite well. Whitehead says of these competing theories that since they were formulated both have had their "periods of triumph." [38]

One might almost say that to the degree that a science has made rapid progress, to that extent is it likely to entertain many theories which seek to account for the torrent of new observations flowing in on it. Thus, Robert Oppenheimer, one of our most distinguished physicists, characterized contemporary atomic physicists as follows: "We have at this time the feeling that we are wandering around in fog, somewhere near base camp number 1." He went on to say: "There is a place for many approaches to the [atomic] system, none of which completely exhausts the subject. You need to think of more than one approach, and you need to carry it out, in order to find out everything that you can find out." [39]

Oppenheimer describes this as the "complementary approach" to the

[37] Simon, *Models of Man: Social and Rational*, p. 97 *ff*.

[38] Alfred North Whitehead, *Science and the Modern World* (New York: Macmillan, 1925), p. 48.

[39] Robert Oppenheimer, "Tradition and Discovery," *ACLS Newsletter* (October 1959), 7.

study of atomic systems.[40] The same attitude should prevail in the social sciences. We must learn to live with diversity. We must be willing to give up the security of one model for all, and accept the uncertainty of a world with many competing models. And we do so not only because we are smugly certain that "in the end they will all add up." They may, but we had better not count on it. More likely we will discover, as Oppenheimer tells us they have discovered in physics, that having done one thing "you lose the value of having done the other." Each approach, he tells us, is a whole chapter, and "these chapters are not serial or cumulative."

Nor should we abandon our models altogether. To think we can is a delusion. They will continue to influence our thinking, only without our awareness, and, therefore, without our control. We must accept what Oppenheimer calls certain "brute facts." Every model, every perspective, exacts its full price from those who use it. In Oppenheimer's words: "In order for us to understand anything, we have to fail to perceive a great deal that is there. Knowledge is always purchased at the expense of what might have been seen and learned and was not. . . . It is a condition of knowledge that somehow or other we pick the clues which give us insight into what we are to find out about the world."[41]

Sociologists' models are such clues. They should, therefore, not be confused with the knowledge itself to which they hopefully will lead. But since the world is endlessly diverse, there is room for many models, each a different potential clue to knowledge.

To urge that we hold to a system of open competition between different models of man and society is not to suggest that it makes no difference which one is chosen. Each model has its special time, its "period of triumph." What makes one model suddenly productive, capable of generating studies which, one after another, excite us and spur on our research, is a complex question we cannot go into. Models seem like mines. The rich veins are quickly exhausted. Those who prefer to work in the old diggings still get some ore out, but the yield is meager. Then someone makes a strike elsewhere. A new gold rush is on as everyone dashes to the fresh field. Yet there are always the lone prospectors, following odd maps, poking around in seemingly unpromising country, one of whom may nevertheless make the next great strike.

To have too many models may, of course, be as bad as being restricted to only one. We then exchange a narrow prison cell for the soaring Tower of Babel. It is not the uses of models, however, but their abuses which should most concern us. Sociologists tend toward dogged intellectual loyalties, favoring one or another approach to the exclusion of all others. The models they prefer often become Procrustean beds from which they blithely hack away all observations which do not fit, or racks on which the facts are tortuously stretched until they take the form the model says they should have.

We must be careful to distinguish between the selective focusing of attention induced by following a particular model, and the distortion of facts perceived under its influence. Selective perception is inevitable, and probably desirable. Without it not only art, but science, could not exist. Distorted perception, however, is a more serious matter. Darwin long ago warned that false observations are a greater danger to scientific advance than false theories. Social scientists tend to an alarming degree to merely derive or deduce alleged

[40] In physics it has some special connotations which need not concern us.
[41] Oppenheimer, "Tradition and Discovery," p. 15.

facts directly from their models rather than to uncover the facts by more or less independent observation. And since checking alleged social facts is a long, laborious, and often unrewarding task, social scientists seldom produce the sort of crucial experiment which really settles an issue. Cohen and Nagel made the point very effectively when they said: "the physical sciences can be more liberal because we are sure that foolish opinions will be readily eliminated by the shock of facts. In the social field, however, no one can tell what harm may come of foolish ideas before the foolishness is finally, if ever, demonstrated." [42]

The solution, however, is not to discard our models. It lies in learning to couch the propositions derived from them in terms which admit of their being objectively tested by the general rules of the game established by science.

[42] Morris Cohen and Ernest Nagel, *An Introduction to Logic and Scientific Method*, abr. ed. (London: Routledge, 1939), p. 239.

four

conceptions of man in sociological analysis[1]

It is inevitable that each sociologist should have some conception of the nature of man, and it is highly probable that it will influence his approach to social research. Yet there is prevalent in sociology a strong resistance to attempts to analyze social phenomena in a way that takes explicit account of psychological factors in social life.

Those who take this position do so, of course, with the most authoritative of sanctions, since it was Durkheim's explicit purpose, in the first great modern work in sociology, to demonstrate that suicide rates could not be explained by individual psychology. As he defined his task in *Suicide*, it was "to determine the productive causes of suicide directly. . . . Disregarding the individual as such, his motives and his ideas." And, again, after reviewing the psychological and other theories on suicide, he declared: "Wholly different are the results we obtained when we forgot the individual and sought the causes of the suicidal aptitude of each society in the nature of the societies themselves . . . the social suicide-rate can be explained only sociologically." [2]

Durkheim was fighting to press back the waters of a veritable sea of

[1] In developing this chapter I have drawn heavily upon my article "Personality and Social Structure," in Robert K. Merton, Leonard Broom, and Leonard S. Cottrell, Jr. (eds.), *Sociology Today* (New York: Basic Books, 1959), pp. 249–276.

[2] Emile Durkheim (J. A. Spaulding and G. Simpson, trans.), *Suicide* (Glencoe, Ill.: The Free Press, 1951), pp. 151, 299.

psychologism in order to expose beneath the surface the solid ledge of societal factors and to create an awareness of the explicit and distinctively social attributes of situations which generated suicide. Considering the difficulty he faced, it may be that the only course open to him was to insist on the exclusive relevance of social factors.

Although Durkheim's position was appropriate for his time, it is a liability for contemporary sociology. It seems clear today that an adequate sociological analysis of many problems is either impossible or severely limited unless we make explicit use of psychological theory and data. Indeed, it may be argued that very little sociological analysis is actually done without using at least an implicit theory about the nature of human personality. In making this theory explicit and bringing psychological data to bear systematically on sociological problems, we cannot fail but improve the scope and adequacy of sociological analysis.

The student of a social structure seeks to explain the implications for social action of a particular set of institutional arrangements. In order to do this, he must correctly estimate the meaning of those arrangements for, or their effect on, the human personality. All institutional arrangements are ultimately mediated through individual action. The consequences of any institutional arrangement, therefore, depend, at least in part, upon its effect on the human personality, broadly conceived. The personality system thus becomes one of the main intervening variables in any estimate of the effects of one aspect of social structure on another. Moreover, since social positions are filled by individuals whose psychic properties may vary, it is likely that the quality of performance of social roles will vary greatly depending on the personality needs and dispositions of those who fill the positions.

Discussions of human nature and society usually focus on themes already discussed by the Greeks: What is the basic nature of man, is he good or evil, socially responsible or a self-centered egotist? How much of what we find in man is inborn, how much a product of his environment? What, if any, are the universal qualities or components of the human personality? How do the traits commonly found in men combine to form the distinctive character we find only in certain men? In what places and under what conditions do these different types emerge and even predominate?

On the Nature of Man

Since sociologists take society as their main concern, and, for the most part, leave the individual to psychology, one does not find among them so wide a range of models of man as of society. While most sociologists make their model of society explicit, their view of man is more often only implicit. Nevertheless, that implicit conception exercises at least as great an influence on their work.

Non-sociological Conceptions

The conception of man held by most sociologists is best understood if we see the contrast between it and other images to which it is often opposed. Among humanists, the most popular view of man stresses his uniqueness, his diversity, the constant change in his mood and perspective, as in Montaigne's remark that man is "a marvelous, vain, fickle and unstable subject, on whom it is hard to form any certain and uniform judgement." [3]

[3] Pitirim A. Sorokin, *Fads and Foibles in Modern Sociology and Related Sciences* (Chicago: Regnery, 1959), p. 59.

By contrast, most sociologists stress the regularity of man's behavior, the repetition of certain socially relevant actions, and the resulting orderliness and calculability of social life which follows from this. The sociologist thus calls attention to man as a creature of social habit. If man were indeed as many humanists depict him, so sociologists argue, we could have none of our familiar institutions nor indeed any organized social life at all.

While psychoanalysis does not emphasize man's ever changing, evanescent quality, it hardly would nominate the social impulse as the tendency most regularly manifested in human behavior. Rather, it sees man as dominated by deep-seated biological drives, by voracious instinctual appetites, which are constantly clamoring for satisfaction. This conception puts man over against society. It considers him as only a weakly restrained animal whose basic primitive nature may at any moment break through in socially disruptive behavior. Freud summed up this view in a letter to Dr. Van Eeden as follows:

> Psychoanalysis has concluded . . . that the primitive, savage, and evil impulses of mankind have not vanished in any individual, but continue their existence, although in repressed state—in the unconscious . . . —and that they wait for opportunities to display their activity.
>
> It has furthermore taught us that our intellect is a feeble and dependent thing, a plaything and tool of our impulses and emotions; that all of us are forced to behave cleverly or stupidly according as our attitudes and inner resistances ordain.[4]

We may note still a third widespread conception of man, sometimes called the Hobbesian view. In this scheme it is not instinctual sexual energy, but social drives of a self-centered sort, which dominate man. He seeks to secure for himself, or for his group, as much wealth, power, and prestige as he possibly can, and cares for no man except as he may be either a necessary condition for, or source of, those personal satisfactions which drive every man. The picture of the world which emerges is one dominated by force and fraud, in which every man is enemy to every other man. In this view only the power of the state prevents the war of each against all and all against each.

These three conceptions hardly begin to cover the range of important images of man contained in Western, let alone world, political philosophy, but they will suffice for our purpose as representative views against which we may set the elements of the most prevalent sociological conception of man.

The Over-socialized Conception of Man

In opposition to the picture of instinctual and irrational man, sociologists put their view of social man, a creature whose animal instincts are tamed and transformed by the process of socialization.[5] There may, perhaps, have been feral children, raised by animals. But if we are to trust the reports, they seemed more animal than human, and seldom survived in civilization for more than a few years. Most sociologists hold that man as we find him everywhere, even in the most primitive tribes, has had his original, raw, animal nature overlaid by a long process of social learning. This directs his biological drives along socially acceptable channels, and indeed often transforms instinctual energies into social impulses of the highest and most selfless sort.

[4] Quoted in Ernest Jones, *The Life and Work of Sigmund Freud*, Vol. II (New York: Basic Books, 1957), p. 368.

[5] The concept of socialization is defined and discussed more fully in Chap. 5.

Sociologists seldom deny the irrational component in man's makeup. Indeed, some sociologists, such as Pareto, have given the problem of the irrational in man's behavior the central place in their scheme of analysis. By and large, however, sociologists do not feel that man's irrationality is quite the obstacle to social life many suppose it to be. They stress society's capacity to prevent its manifestation, or through sanctions to control its effects. They emphasize man's persistent and purposeful pursuit of the social and personal goals which his culture and time define as appropriate. In this sense most human action is "rational," and in the sociological view, were it not so, men could hardly survive in nature. Men could not for certain count on the action of other men, and social life would be all but impossible. And since men are mutually dependent on others for existence, human life itself would disappear.

Opposed to the Hobbesian image of man as isolated, exaggeratedly self-centered, and extremely individuated, sociologists more often see man mainly in terms of his social drives. They emphasize his desire and need for affiliation and companionship, this dependence on others for cooperation and assistance, his interest in extending his personally limited resources and power through group action. In the common sociological image, man values others and seeks to relate himself to them. He is seen as committed to mutual adaptation and adjustment to attain not only his individual and private ends but also the communal and public goals which he has *internalized* and made his own.

Certain elements, then, stand out in the sociological conception of man, of which we may note three: Man's "*original nature*" is seen largely in neutral terms, as neither good nor bad. It is, rather, a potential for development, and the extent to which the potential is realized depends on the time and society into which a man is born and on his distinctive place in it. If it does not quite treat him as a "tabula rasa," modern sociology, nevertheless, regards man as a flexible form which can be given all manner of content.

Socialization, the process of learning one's culture while growing out of infant and childhood dependency, leads to internalization of society's values and goals. People come to want to do what from the point of society they must do. Man is, therefore, seen, in his inner being, as mainly moral, by and large accepting and fulfilling the demands society makes on him.

In his external life, in relations with his fellows, man is seen as social man. Locked into a network of social relationships, dependent on others for support and cooperation, eager to earn their good will and approbation, he responds to external pressures which again push him to act mainly in accord with the norms and standards characteristic of society in his time and place.

These three elements, which make up the typical sociological image of man, have been dubbed by Dennis Wrong as "the over-socialized conception of man." [6] If we trace the relation of this conception to theories in Western political philosophy, we must acknowledge that it bears striking resemblance to the image of man contained in the thinking of the Enlightenment, to the tradition of Locke and Rousseau, of Montesquieu and John Stuart Mill. It has much less in common, indeed must generally be seen as opposed to, the view of man proposed by Machiavelli, Hobbes, Hume, and Kant. It also is obviously a view more congruent with the structural-functional

[6] Dennis Wrong, "The Oversocialized Conception of Man," *American Sociological Review* (1961), XXVI:183–192.

approach, especially the equilibrium model, than with the conflict model of society.

We are not seeking here to assess the correctness or adequacy of this image, but only the consequences of holding it. Taking the view of human nature which they do, sociologists must be expected to reject the idea that differences between nations or cultures are in important degree caused by innate differences in the people of different countries. They will much more likely look to differences in level of material culture and in the forms of economic, political, and social organization to explain the behavior of different nations.

In the study of differences within any population, sociologists are likely to be found ranged against those who explain crime, juvenile delinquency, suicide, or the like, on the basis of innate differences in individuals or groups. Instead, sociologists propose to explain these phenomena as products of social arrangements which impinge with differential force on certain individuals because of the distinctive position they occupy in the social structure.[7] Because they thus minimize man's inherent propensities to evil, the explanations they offer of starker phenomena such as mass murder, war, mob action, inquisitions, concentration camps, and the like, tend to be weak and pale alongside those offered by other disciplines such as psychology or history.

Finally, the sociologists' conception of human nature leads them to believe that to change man we must first change social conditions, rather than the reverse. At the same time they are likely to be very dubious of reforms which promise utopian conditions under which man will at last be fully free and subject to no social restraints whatever. They rather take their stand on a middle ground. While holding that man's anti-social and self-centered impulses can either be restrained or channeled to serve the public good, they acknowledge that in the process man must inevitably suffer some important restraints on the free and untrammeled expression of his impulses. Despite these restraints, sociologists argue, on balance social life leaves man infinitely more free for development and self-expression than he could be in any conceivable unsocialized state of nature.

Types of Men in Sociology

In the past a great deal of sociological energy was invested in devising typologies of personality as a way of explaining the differences in behavior characteristic of different societies and of important groups within the same society. In *The Polish Peasant*, one of the landmarks of sociological research, W. I. Thomas and F. Znaniecki described the Bohemian, the Philistine, and the Creative Man. Park and Stonequist gave us "the marginal man," William Whyte the "street corner boy," Paul Lazarsfeld the "opinion-leaders," and Robert Merton the "cosmopolitans" and the "locals." [8] The pattern seems so compelling that even the popularizers of sociology have

[7] For a fuller exposition of this point see the discussion of sociological studies of deviance and conformity in Chap. 6.

[8] W. I. Thomas and Florian Znaniecki, *The Polish Peasant in Europe and America*, Vol. I–IV (Chicago: University of Chicago Press, 1918); E. V. Stonequist, *The Marginal Man: A Study in Personality and Culture Conflict* (New York: Scribner, 1937); William F. Whyte, *Street Corner Society, the Social Structure of an Italian Slum* (Chicago: University of Chicago Press, 1943); Paul Lazarsfeld, Bernard Berelson, and Hazel Gaudet, *The People's Choice* (New York: Duell, Sloan and Pearce, 1944); Robert K. Merton, "Patterns of Influence: Local and Cosmopolitan Influentials," *Social Theory and Social Structure*, rev. and enl. ed. (Glencoe, Ill.: The Free Press, 1957), pp. 387–420.

followed suit, as Vance Packard did in calling his book on social stratification *The Status Seekers*. Since the delineation of socio-psychological types seems so pervasive and important in sociological analysis, we should understand it more fully. Two illustrations will perhaps facilitate the process.

Vilfredo Pareto created one of the most distinctive and imposing systems of sociology.[9] One of the central elements in his system was the concept of "residues," by which he meant the rather elemental and enduring qualities of social action. He regarded the residues as "constants" in human behavior. A given residue might be characteristic of a particular society, institution, or person. Pareto distinguished six main classes of residues, and he characterized different societies, times, groups, and persons according to the residues which were most characteristic of them. For example, he spoke of "foxes," people in whom "residues of combination" were strong. "Foxes" innovate, experiment, take risks. A speculator is typical of the "foxes." By contrast, the "lions" are more traditional, devoted to routine and fixed ways of doing things, and lacking in imagination. In them the strong residue is that of "the persistence of aggregates," and they are typified by the *rentier*.

Pareto used this conception of social types and their underlying characteristics to explain both social stability and social change. He held that ideally a society should have leadership strong in the "residues of combination," and followers strong in the residues of "persistence of aggregates." In most historical cases, Pareto argued, the ruling classes are not flexible enough to absorb into their ranks those of the lower classes displaying leadership qualities. This leads to revolution, and replacement of the old elite with new groups high in the residues of combination. Then the cycle resumes in an endless "circulation of elites." Pareto thus used the idea of social types, each bearing different residues, as a basis for what we have defined as a cyclical theory of social evolution.[10]

In *The Lonely Crowd* David Riesman presents a different set of social types, one which has probably achieved wider currency than any sociological typology ever attained.[11] Riesman distinguished three main types, each of which represents a different model of conformity, or of response to social control.

The "tradition-directed" are those whose behavior is minutely controlled from without by traditional cultural standards, by kinship ties, religion, ceremonials, and the like. Their outstanding characteristic is conformity to the external standards of behavior, the etiquette of their community. "Inner-directed" people are responsive not to "strict and self-evident tradition," but rather to standards "implanted early in life by the elders and directed toward generalized but nonetheless inescapably destined goals." [12] They are the men with a gyroscope inside. By contrast, the "other-directed" are individuals for whom their contemporaries are the source of direction.[13] They follow the crowd.

Riesman called these "historic" types because he feels that each is most characteristic of a given kind of society at a certain stage of development. The tradition-directed man is typical in long settled, unchanging societies,

[9] Vilfredo Pareto (T. Livingston, ed.), *Mind, Self and Society*, Vol. I–IV (New York: Harcourt Brace & World, 1939). For commentary see George C. Homans and Charles D. Curtis, *An Introduction to Pareto: His Sociology* (New York: Knopf, 1934).

[10] See also the section on social change in Chap. 6.

[11] David Riesman, *The Lonely Crowd*, abr. (New York: Doubleday, 1958); see also S. Martin Lipset and Leo Lowenthal, *Culture and Social Character* (Glencoe, Ill.: The Free Press, 1961).

[12] Riesman, *The Lonely Crowd*, p. 30.

[13] *Ibid.*, p. 31 *ff*.

where there is a fairly stable ratio of man-to-land, combined with great potential for growth in the unused reserves of the society. In Western history the Middle Ages may be regarded as a period high in tradition-direction.

According to Riesman, a change in the ratio of births to deaths often brings about profound changes in such a traditional society. As the population expands, the death rate drops, agriculture improves and yields surpluses, and a new character type comes forward to take advantage of new opportunities. These are periods of rapid social mobility, of the accumulation of capital, of invention and expansion. In such times the inner-directed man comes to the fore. The Renaissance and the Reformation are periods in our history which were ideally suited to the rise of the inner-directed man.

Further changes in society, according to the theory, bring further changes in the dominant social type. Death rates follow birth rates downward; population becomes static or declines; agriculture is replaced by industry, and industry in part by the service occupations; hours are short, materials and leisure abundant. At such times men find that: "Increasingly, *other people* are the problem, not the material environment." [14] This is the period in which the other-directed type rises to prominence. The United States after World War II may serve as an example.

It is evident from the use Pareto and Riesman make of their typologies that developing them was not just an amusing parlor game. They used the character types in historical perspective to illumine major social processes of adjustment and change. But it is also apparent from these illustrations that the method provides a rather shaky basis on which to rest a structure of sociological analysis. Almost every time we turn around, another sociologist has come forward with a new set of social types. Whose character types shall we then accept as authentic and socially important?

On closer examination the types defined by different authors seem often to be the same old cast of characters decked out with new and catching titles, even though the historic plot is basically unchanged and even the parts sound fundamentally the same. Riesman's tradition-directed man, for example, seems very much like those whom Pareto characterized as strong in the residues of "persistence of aggregates," and we would not have to meet him in the dark to confuse the inner-directed man with the fellow high on the "aggregates of combination." These types are also very similar to those described by Thomas and Znaniecki, and Riesman himself acknowledges that the inner-directed man is very much like Max Weber's bearer of "the Protestant ethic." [15]

There is an appropriate resolution of the difficulty. The inventors of the social types might be asked to define more precisely exactly what are the signs, the indicators, whereby we might know one type from another. Unfortunately, we often discover on closer examination that the distinguishing characteristics of the types cannot be precisely stated. The other-directed, for example, is supposed to be typically influenced by his contemporaries. Yet it is obvious that both the tradition-directed and inner-directed must also be somewhat influenced by contemporaries if they live successfully in society. We, therefore, want to know how much each is influenced by his contemporaries, and in which realms of life this influence is more important—in the choice of one's car, the books one reads, the wife one takes, the profession one pursues?

Such questions lead to another issue—that of empirical substantiation.

[14] *Ibid.*, p. 34.
[15] *Ibid.*, p. 33.

Even if we can be sure that the separate qualities Pareto and Riesman describe actually exist in real men, how do we know whether they in fact combine in the way the authors imagine? And even if the separate qualities do hold together in the way the sociologist imagines, how can we tell whether these types are actually found in the social groups of which they are believed to be typical? What evidence do we have, for example, that Riesman is correct in his assertion that other-directed people seem to be emerging distinctively in the upper-middle classes of our larger cities, and more prominently in New York than in Boston?

To answer such questions we need reliable and valid measures of the qualities which presumably characterize the various social types. With such measures we could, at least in a contemporary setting, directly test sub-groups, or the total populations, of different nations selected as representative of the various stages of development described by Riesman. Analysis of the results would indicate whether his hypotheses were correct, and would give us some measure of the usefulness of his social types as a tool of sociological analysis.

Until very recently the suggestion that we undertake such research would have been utopian. We did not know how to devise the necessary tests, we had no means to apply them, and no way to test their value if the results could have been obtained. Anyone was, therefore, quite safe in proposing yet another set of social types to explain both history and contemporary events.

The situation is today quite different. A long line of technological advances has given sociologists and psychologists the ability to devise tests of character, to apply them by sampling methods to large groups of people, and through statistics to meaningfully analyze the results and relate them to other aspects of social structure. Perhaps the most notable early effort of this sort was made by Gordon Allport and Phillip Vernon. They devised a test of values to distinguish the 6 types of men suggested by the German social psychologist E. Spranger, who delineated the theoretical, economic, social, religious, and political types.[16] Several people are at work seeking to devise objective tests of the personality types described by David Riesman.[17] It is interesting that these empirical studies, although done by people sympathetic to Riesman, seem to encounter some of the difficulties our theoretical analysis above anticipated. For example, a study of 2,500 9th- and 10th-grade students by the Rileys failed to locate the inner- and other-directed as pure types. In most students both of these elements were found to be of more or less equal strength.[18]

Perhaps the most outstanding instance of success among the efforts to develop systematic empirical measures of a theoretically important personality type is found in studies of the authoritarian personality. This concept was developed by the psychoanalyst Erich Fromm on the basis of his psychiatric

[16] Edward Spranger (P. J. W. Pigers, trans.), *Types of Men: The Psychology and Ethics of Personality*, 5th ed. (Halle M. Niemeyer, 1928); Gordon Allport, P. Vernon, and G. Lindzey, *Manual: Study of Values—a Scale for Measuring the Dominant Interests in Personality*, 3rd ed. (Boston: Houghton, Mifflin, 1960).

[17] For example, see Robert Gutman and Dennis Wrong, "David Riesman's Typology of Character," pp. 295–315; Elaine G. Sofer, "Inner-Direction, Other-Direction and Autonomy," pp. 316–348; and Matilda White Riley, John W. Riley, and Mary E. Moore, "Adolescent Values and the Riesman Typology," pp. 370–388, all in Lipset and Lowenthal (eds.), *Culture and Social Character*.

[18] Riley, *et al.*, in Lipset and Lowenthal (eds.), *Culture and Social Character*, pp. 370–388.

practice and study of history. Later a group of clinical psychologists studied the problem intensely in one of the most complex, thorough, and important social science investigations of the mid-century.[19] Their approach combined careful study of documents, psychological testing, depth interviewing, and a review of individual behavior. They established conclusively that there was a syndrome of psychological traits which, in combination, they called "authoritarianism." Included in this syndrome were extreme conventionality; "anti-intraceptivity," meaning resistance to looking inside oneself to examine one's feelings, emotions, and impulses; a tendency to project onto others one's "bad" impulses, especially in regard to sex; and a feeling that authority is absolute and one must be submissive to it. From a sociological point of view one outcome of great importance was the development of a fairly simple pencil-and-paper questionnaire, known as the F scale, which permits quick and easy scoring of an individual's authoritarian tendencies.

The F scale is representative of a newer form of psychological test which is so easy to give and score that it can be economically and effectively administered to large samples as part of a general public-opinion survey. As a result of such developments we now can locate with considerable accuracy the positions in the social structure in which one or another psychological type is more frequently found. For example, in the national sample of the American people in which the F scale was used, Janowitz and Marvick found only 13 per cent of the well-educated members of the upper-middle class scored high on authoritarianism. This quality was much more prevalent in the lower class, being evident in some 30 per cent of the cases. But interestingly enough, the greatest concentration of persons high on authoritarianism was among those who held white-collar jobs but had low incomes or little education. In this group almost 40 per cent scored high. Janowitz and Marvick concluded, therefore, that their empirical study gave support to the theory, expounded in many contemporary analyses, that this group is particularly susceptible to authoritarianism because of the frustrations its members experience in their striving to achieve middle-class status.[20]

The development of simple pencil-and-paper tests of personality such as the F scale opens the possibility that at last we can provide scientific answers to one of the oldest and most troublesome questions in the study of man: "Are there basic differences in the character or personality of the people who make up the different nations of the world? The concept of national character is not only old, but has long been under attack for its presumed kinship with discredited theories about racial psychology. However eager they may be to avoid seeming to be prejudiced, let alone being "racists," social scientists cannot avoid dealing systematically with the issue now that it becomes practically possible to deal with it empirically.

There are grave technical difficulties facing those who would use psychological tests across national boundaries. But with sufficient inventiveness and proper precautions they may sensibly be used. Optimism, or at least the public expression of happiness, has been measured in a number of comparative polls of public opinion in the Western World. Invariably the French

[19] T. W. Adorno, *et al., The Authoritarian Personality* (New York: Harper, 1950), see especially Chapter VII. See also Richard Christie and Marie Jahoda (eds.), *Studies in Scope and Method of 'The Authoritarian Personality'* (Glencoe, Ill.: The Free Press, 1954). This book contains the contributions of six social scientists who criticize and comment upon the methodological and theoretical aspects of *The Authoritarian Personality*, and consider its impact and implications for studies in the field.

[20] Morris Janowitz and D. Marvick, "Authoritarianism and Political Behavior," *Public Opinion Quarterly* (1953), XVII:185–201.

emerge as the particularly dour or pessimistic. As many as 40 per cent describe themselves as "not very happy," whereas in other countries of Europe only about 10 per cent are quite so negative. By contrast, the people of the United States score very high on these measures. For example, 43 per cent of the Americans reported themselves "very happy," compared to only 11 per cent of the French.[21]

The F scale has also been used cross-nationally with good results, at least within the limits of continental Europe. Administered to school teachers in 7 countries, the scale seemed to "work" much as it does in the United States.[22] There were clear differences in the average score of the several national samples, and in the expected direction, with England and Sweden showing significantly less authoritarianism than Germany. But the differences *between* countries were not much greater than the differences *within* countries when teachers were grouped by religious affiliation. Catholics generally scored higher than Protestants, and both religious groups showed more authoritarian tendencies than those claiming no religious affiliation.

Not only the nations of today but even the societies of the past may prove to be accessible to the students of national character. David McClelland applied the same type of measure used to rate individuals on their "need for achievement" in order to score written materials from earlier epochs in Ancient Greece, Spain in the Middle Ages, England in the period before the Industrial Revolution, and the United States between 1800 and 1950. Indeed, even cultures which left no written record, such as pre-Inca Peru, can be rated on "need for achievement" by applying to the designs on pottery a scoring system originally used with the "doodles" of living persons. Again these efforts are plagued by a host of technical difficulties, but the relations McClelland found between changes in the economic activity of societies and the average amount of achievement imagery in their literature and pottery strongly suggests that such procedures for rating the psychological properties of past eras may be quite feasible and reasonably reliable.[23]

We are only on the edge of a great field of exploration. Our early experience indicates, as is almost always the case, that social reality is more complex than our initial schemes suggest, and the key to social change more elusive than we imagined. The pure qualities of personality dealt with by theory—such as Pareto's risk-taking and innovation or Riesman's "responsiveness to contemporaries"—are elusive, hard to measure, and difficult to isolate in real situations. Often the composite ideal types cannot be found. In reality the pure components of personal psychology may combine differently from the way the men who invented them imagined they would. We are just beginning to learn where, in a population such as that of the United States, the different psychological types are most frequently found. Comparative studies simultaneously conducted in several countries are still largely for the future. Nevertheless, there is no doubt that we are on the verge of important advances in systematic studies of the socially defined personality types prevalent at various times and in various social roles. How far we can apply this approach to the past is uncertain. But on the basis of

[21] These and other comparable results of cross-national opinion polls will be found in Alex Inkeles, "Industrial Man," *American Journal of Sociology* (1960), LXVI:1–31.

[22] From an unpublished study by Daniel J. Levinson, Arthur S. Couch, and Stein Rokan, based on material obtained by the Organization for Comparative Social Research.

[23] David C. McClelland, *The Achieving Society* (Princeton: D. Von Nostrand, 1961), especially Chap. IV, "Achieving Societies in the Past."

such studies in the future, we may come to a firmer and more substantial knowledge of the role which the different types of personality play in social change.

Personality in Social Roles

If pressed to do so, most sociologists will certainly acknowledge that in principle sociological analysis must keep in mind the nature of human personality, and will grant that personality factors theoretically may play a substantial role in determining individual social behavior. But they are also likely to be rather dubious that such factors possess anything like the influence exerted by more "objective" structural forces or the individual's social position as described in terms of occupation, education, income, and the like. It is highly relevant to our purpose, therefore, to consider how more systematic use of psychological theory and personality data have contributed to a deeper understanding of a problem of major sociological importance—namely, recruitment to occupational and other status-positions and the quality of role performance.[24]

Sociologists have traditionally explained the fact that most people fulfill their major social obligations by referring to the system of sanctions imposed on those who fail to meet, and the rewards granted to those who do meet, the expectations of society. Performance is thus seen as largely dependent on factors "outside" the person. The only thing that need be posited as "inside," in this view, is the general desire to avoid punishment and to gain rewards. Important as such "drives" may be, they do not seem sufficient to explain the differences in the way people perform their assigned social roles. While accepting the crucial importance of the objective factors which determine social behavior, we must recognize that recruitment into occupational and other status-positions, and the quality of performance in the roles people are thus assigned, may, to an important degree, be influenced by personal qualities in individuals. It may be assumed, further, that this happens on a sufficiently large scale to be a crucial factor in determining the functioning of any social system. To the degree that this is true, to predict the functioning of a particular institution, of a small- or large-scale system, we need to know not only the system of status-positions but also the distribution of personality characteristics in the population at large and among those playing important roles in the system.

It would not do justice to the facts to say that sociologists give no consideration to the commonly observed and often marked behavioral characteristics of the incumbents of certain occupations. They generally assume, however, that these characteristics emerge as a response to the distinctive situational—or as they say "structural"—pressures which one typically encounters on the particular job. In other words, they assume "anybody" would probably respond the same way, and that the personality types one encounters in certain positions probably got that way as a result of the job. This point of view is reflected in an influential article by Robert Merton, first published in 1949, on the relation of personality and bureaucracy. With great skill Merton shows how the values and pressures on the employees of large-scale organizations induce them in the very process of conscientiously fulfilling their duties to engage in that sort of exaggerated behavior we label disparagingly as "bureaucratic." As Merton puts it: "As a result of their day

[24] These concepts—status-position and role—are defined and discussed in Chap. 5.

to day routines, people develop special preferences, antipathies, discriminations and emphases." [25] In other words, the bureaucratic personality is learned on the job.

Although Merton emphasized almost exclusively how the job shapes the person, he did, at the very end of his article, raise the question whether or not organizations do not in fact *select* a particular personality type.[26]

As sociologists and psychologists turned, in the post-war period, to a more systematic examination of this question, substantial evidence accumulated to show that people are indeed differentially attracted to occupations on the basis of their personality characteristics. Perhaps the most substantial evidence comes from a study of the occupational preference of a nation-wide sample of American college students who were asked to indicate their choice of career and to reply to a series of questions which made it possible to score their values, personality, and social characteristics. The study yielded much evidence of very strong influence exerted by personality on the students' career plans. For example, those who scored high on a test of "faith in people" were much more likely to prefer professions in which one gives personal service. Thus, of those who planned to be social workers, 62 per cent had high faith, whereas among those who planned to enter sales or promotional work, only 22 per cent so responded. Those who were classified as "detached" personalities chose professions involving little contact with others—such as art, architecture, and natural science—twice as often as did those who were classified as either "aggressive" or "compliant" personalities. With the passage of time in college, furthermore, more and more of the students brought their occupational choice into line with their values by changing to more appropriate occupations. Among one group of Cornell undergraduates, for example, the co-efficient of association between values and career choice increased from .559 in 1950 to .711 in 1952.[27]

It is of the utmost relevance for the main point we are making in this section to compare the relative influence on career choice exercised by personality factors as against objective indices such as fathers' occupation and income. Although the research report did not directly compare the power of these two influences, the data presented suggest that such structural factors exert only equal and perhaps even weaker influence on career choice than did the value and personality factors.

Whether arising from differential recruitment or developed on the job, differences in modal personality type in different occupations are relevant to the sociologist only if they can be shown to affect individual role performance and, consequently, institutional functioning. Studies in which data on personality and on role performance are simultaneously reported are rare. The few available indicate that personality does have a marked influence on role performance. In a study of nurses' aides in a mental hospital, Gilbert and Levinson obtained both a measure of personality and a measure of role performance. The aspect of personality they studied was authoritarianism, as measured by the famous F scale, and the evaluation of objective behavior was based on the reports of the aides' supervisors. Gilbert and Levinson rated the aides as "custodial" or "humanistic" on the basis of their treatment of patients. Aides were considered "custodial" in behavior if they made

[25] Robert K. Merton, "Bureaucratic Structure and Personality," *Social Theory and Social Structure*, p. 198.

[26] *Ibid*., p. 205 *ff*.

[27] Morris Rosenberg, *Occupations and Values* (Glencoe, Ill.: The Free Press, 1957), p. 20 *ff*.

many threats to patients and placed prime emphasis on keeping the wards quiet. They were scored as "humanistic" if they were more friendly and respectful toward the patients and assumed the role of "social" therapist for their wards. For the female aides in three Boston hospitals, the rank-order correlation between custodialism in the treatment of patients and score on authoritarianism in personality was .75, reflecting an extremely strong influence of personality on behavior on the job.[28]

Several outstanding studies relate personality to school performance. Stern, Stein, and Bloom obtained a series of performance measures for two groups, each of 61 college students, who were rated high and low on stereopathy. The stereopathic personality, broadly similar to the authoritarian, is one who accepts authority as absolute and is submissive to it, prefers depersonalized and "codified" relations with other people, inclines to rigid orderliness and conformity, and usually inhibits or denies his psychic impulses.[29] The importance of these traits is evident when we learn that the emphasis at the college concerned, presumably at the University of Chicago, was placed on "capacity for detachment, for delaying resolution or closure, and for tolerating ambiguous relativities rather than demanding structural absolutes." [30] The college thus placed a premium on qualities which were characteristic of nonstereopaths and relatively lacking in those personalities high in stereopathy.

Striking differences emerged in the college performance of the two personality types. At the end of the first year, 23 per cent of the stereopathic students had withdrawn from the college, whereas only 1 per cent of the nonstereopaths had done so.[31] Intelligence made virtually no difference in this performance. The complaints of the withdrawing stereopathic students strongly suggested that their action resulted from a lack of congruence between their personality and their consequent ambitions and hopes, on the one hand, and the special requirements of the particular college they had entered, on the other. They complained most about the seeming lack of discipline, the refusal of instructors to give the "right" answers, and the separation between course content and their immediate and practical vocational interests.[32] This outcome was largely as had been predicted from an examination of the distinctive qualities of education at the particular college and the distinctive personality attributes of the stereopathic students.

It is clear from these studies that recruitment to status-positions and subsequent role performance cannot safely be predicted solely on the basis of the extrinsic features of a position and its place in the larger social structure. The personalities of those occupying status-positions strongly influence the quality of their performance. And since it seems likely that personalities are not randomly recruited to social positions, the effects of the modal personality patterns in any given group of job incumbents may strongly influence the performance of the group as a whole. We see then that both social structure and personality must be treated as important independent, but interacting, variables influencing the flow of the social process.

[28] Doris C. Gilbert and Daniel J. Levinson, "Role Performance, Ideology and Personality in Mental Hospital Aides," in Milton Greenblatt, *et al.* (eds.), *The Patient and the Mental Hospital* (Glencoe, Ill.: The Free Press, 1957), p. 206.

[29] George C. Stern, Morris J. Stein, and Benjamin S. Bloom, *Methods in Personality Assessment* (Glencoe, Ill.: The Free Press, 1956), p. 189.

[30] *Ibid.*, p. 206.

[31] *Ibid.*, p. 210.

[32] *Ibid.*, p. 213.

Personality and Politics

Systematic studies which attempt to show how personality influences recruitment to status-positions and later role performance can be extended far beyond the limits of the more restricted study of occupations. We are just beginning to grasp in a more systematic way how personality factors influence the choice of political role and the style of political action.[33] For example, Henry Dicks, a British psychiatrist, was able to demonstrate a strong relationship in German prisoners of war between their personality dispositions and their orientation to Naziism. Those classified *politically* as "fanatical, wholehearted Nazis," when compared with politically anti-Nazi German soldiers on the basis of psychiatric interviews, were judged to show a marked taboo against tenderness, to be more sadistic, and to be more likely to engage in "projection" as a psychic defense.[34]

The development of psychological measures which can be administered in the form of questionnaires permits us to extend this type of analysis to large samples and to a variety of political processes under more natural conditions than those confronting Dr. Dicks. In their study of authoritarianism in the American population, for example, Janowitz and Marvick found that authoritarianism was strongly related to whether or not people bothered to vote. Of the non-voters, 40 per cent scored high on the personality measure of authoritarianism (F scale), whereas among those who voted in the preceding elections only 25 per cent were so classified.[35] F scale scores were also strongly related to the position people took on foreign policy. Among those high on authoritarianism, 45 per cent favored a strongly isolationist position, whereas among the low scorers only 22 per cent took an isolationist stand on U.S. foreign policy.[36] We should note a parallel between this study and one on student values. The personality measure was as effective in predicting voting behavior and foreign policy preferences as were the more objective structural indices usually emphasized by sociologists, such as income and education.

Personality and Social Structure

I have argued that sociological analysis—the attempt to understand the structure and functioning of social systems—will often require the use of a general theory of personality and knowledge of the distinctive personality characteristics of participants in the system as a whole, in major sub-systems, and in particular status-positions. To many, this may suggest that I am proposing a "reduction" of sociological analysis to the presumably more basic level of psychological analysis. I am by no means implying or suggesting this course. What is at issue here is not the reduction of one discipline to another but the articulation of the two for certain specific purposes under certain specific conditions.

The two disciplines have quite different analytic foci. Sociology is the study of the structure and functioning of social systems—that is, relatively enduring systems of action, shared by groups of people, large or small. Psy-

[33] For a fuller account of the problem, see Alex Inkeles, "National Character and Modern Political Systems" in Francis Hsu (ed.), *Psychological Anthropology* (Homewood: Dorsey, 1961), pp. 172–209.

[34] Henry V. Dicks, "Personality Traits and the National Socialist Ideology," *Human Relations* (1950), III:111–154.

[35] Janowitz and Marvick, *Public Opinion Quarterly*, XVII:200.

[36] *Ibid.*, p. 198.

chology is the study of structure and functioning of the personal system—the system of action which characterizes an individual biological organism, notably a human being. There are many areas of traditional sociological research for which personality theory or knowledge of modal personality patterns would seem to have little or no relevance—for example, most demographic research, a substantial part of urban sociology, and a great many problems in measurement or social mapping, including the mapping of class structures.[37] But if we go beyond the mapping of a class structure to deal with the behavior of members of different classes and the rates, say, of stability in or mobility out of the particular classes, then psychological data may assume great importance in the general model of analysis. This is not to say, however, that the problem "reduces" itself to personal psychology. Obviously, in an occupational pyramid with relatively few jobs defined as very desirable and many defined as less desirable, the amount of mobility out of the lower classes is objectively given by the nature of the pyramid. If education of a given level or quality is a prerequisite to attaining certain occupational levels and such education is generally not available in rural areas, the rate of mobility for rural residents will be primarily determined by these facts.

Within the framework of such structurally set limits, however, there is a broad area in which personality forces have considered room to operate. For lack of appropriate motivation, those who are otherwise eligible may not use their opportunities for mobility to maximum advantage. Of those who strive, some will have the capacity, some will not. Even a cursory glance at the many recent studies stimulated by our national need to discover and train inborn talent will reveal the serious miscalculations we have made in assuming that only objective factors of "opportunity" are important in determining mobility drives. If we are to go beyond the mere statistical charting of mobility rates for different strata to more complex explanatory schemes with predictive possibilities in new situations, we must be able to deal with the personal component—the motivated actor in the social situation. The mobility rate for the society is not thus reduced to a matter of mere personal psychology. It remains a social, not a personal, datum.

The same is true of the other aspects of the individual's social context of action. But the actions of individuals in any situation are personal, however much they reflect the determining influence of the social environment. And that environment, in turn, can be reflected in individual action only to the extent that it is mediated through the personal system or personality. A full understanding of any social situation and its probable consequences, therefore, assumes a knowledge not only of the main facts about the social structure—the gathering of which is presumably the special province of sociological study—but also of the main facts about the personalities operating in that structure. Thus, what is required is not a reduction of either mode of analysis to the allegedly more fundamental level of the other, but rather an integration or coordination of two basic sets of data in a larger explanatory scheme.

[37] Social stratification and social mobility are discussed more fully in Chap. 6.

basic elements of social life

five

To meet the challenge posed by the problems of developing, sustaining, and elaborating their life in common, men universally develop specialized activities. The first principle of social life is the division of labor, the elaboration of differentiated actions designed to meet the exigencies of daily living in social conditions. The differentiation and specialization of human activities compels us to develop a set of terms which are appropriately differentiated and sufficiently specialized to do justice to the phenomena we are studying.

Sociologists are often criticized for their use of jargon, their apparent predilection to develop new words while at the same time giving new and often strange meanings to old and familiar terms. The charges are often justified. Equally often they go beyond reason. Systematic discussion is impossible if one does not work with more or less precisely defined terms. Without a technical language, scientific communication becomes cumbersome and inefficient. Even in the humanities, the desire to be more precise in analysis leads to the elaboration of technical terms, as anyone familiar with the "new criticism" in literature will testify.

In point of fact, sociological terminology has been relatively stable, at least as far as many of its core concepts are concerned. As early as 1900, the index of the first major sociological journal, *L'Année Sociologique*, contained many of the terms which are standard in sociological usage today, such as: urban concentration, sect, race, mores, exogamy, family disintegration, social disaggregation, conformism, classes, caste, associations, and adaptation. It is not so much the terms but the disagreement about their definition, the ambiguities of their meaning, and the lack of standardization in their use which are the basic problems in sociology. In this respect sociology presents a sharp contrast to the natural sciences. Nevertheless, most sociologists agree about basic concepts.

However necessary they may be, the definitions of the technical terms in any field are much less interesting than the uses to which the terms are put in analyzing subject matter. Being all too ready to accept this point, I decided against presenting a set of basic sociological concepts and terms in the cut-and-dried form of a glossary or list of definitions. I chose, instead, to introduce these terms gradually in the course of unfolding an approach to man in society, and delineating the problems of analysis which face the sociologist who hopes to enrich our knowledge and deepen our understanding of social processes.

By way of introduction I have briefly sketched the minimum requirements, sometimes called the "prerequisites," of human social existence. These are the conditions which any social unit must meet if life is to be sustained and continued through the generations. The ways in which these prerequisites are satisfied represents what is distinctively *social* action as against that which is human but indistinguishable from the behavior of other mammals. In solving his basic problems of existence, man develops a series of patterns of action considered the basic forms of social organization. These forms range from the simplest customs, such as those governing greetings and departures, through units of intermediate size, complexity, and completeness, such as the community, and culminate in the self-sufficient society, the largest unit for sociological analysis. Cutting across all such units, however, and the common element in all, is the social relationship, which some sociologists feel is the really unique subject matter of sociology. Without necessarily accepting this opinion we may, nevertheless, acknowledge the importance of this perspective. There follows, therefore, a brief discussion of efforts to develop special terms to describe the aspects of any social relationship, as well as some illustrations of efforts to use this approach in research.

The Minimum Requirements of Human Social Life

It is the nature of man that he can and does elaborate many aspects of his life until they achieve a degree of subtlety and complexity beyond all imagining. This tendency is rare, indeed almost completely absent, in the animal and insect world. Animals may have simple means to communicate, as in signaling the presence of enemies or food, but they do not have language which can be used to write elaborate folk tales, create poetry, and fashion novels. Some animals and insects do intricate "dances" but these are rigidly fixed by instinct, are generally invariant, and are highly specific to such acts as mating. Neither animal nor insect develops a repertoire of dances for all occasions, or simply for no occasion other than recreation and pleasure. Birds may build complex nests and spiders weave marvellous webs, but no animals or birds elaborate the building of structures and their decoration so far beyond their immediate need for shelter and for preservation as does man in his architectural fancy.

Man's propensity to elaborate the elements of human action easily obscures the fact that underneath this overlay there is a hard core of basic problems of existence which he must also face. These are not limited to the *physical* survival of the isolated or independent organism. Because men always live in groups, they face a set of fundamental problems of *social* life no less important.

Any living group which endures for several generations has presumably found some way to meet these demands, else it would not have endured so long. If the solutions are relatively imperfect, the society may be functioning poorly, subject to much strain, and perhaps destined to break up if it does not soon find better ones. If the society's answer to the basic challenges of social life are reasonably satisfactory, however, the system may keep going for a long time. Since all "ongoing" social systems are presumably meeting the minimum requirements for existence to some degree, it is easy to take these requirements for granted, and to pass directly on to a discussion of major institutions such as the family. This is unfortunate. The inescapable minimum requirements of social life exert so profound an influence that no conception of society can be complete or even adequate unless it takes account of the role which this set of underlying problems plays in organizing and focusing all social action.

The question we face here is analogous to that posed in biology: What conditions must be met to sustain the life of an organism? The sociological form of the question is: If social life is to persist, what conditions must be met by society? The answer has been couched in various terms. One of the best known of the recent attempts rests on the concept of "the functional prerequisites of any social system." Under this rubric, a group of Talcott Parsons' students proposed a list of some 10 conditions any society must meet, ranging from such obvious needs as that for a common system of communication to rather less self-evident requirements such as that for "the regulation of affective expression." [1]

Although to do so may involve some simplification, we may conveniently group the recurrent problems facing any society in three main sets, each dealing with a different type of adaptation to the basic facts of life.

Adaptation to the external environment, physical and human, lies at the center of the first set of requirements. For a group to survive, it must have a technology adequate to provide some minimum of food, clothing, and shelter appropriate to its size, geographical setting, climate, and the like. In addition to meeting this short-run problem, the group must provide for its long-run survival. This requires, above all, providing nurturing and care for the very young who are unable either to support or to protect themselves. Protection includes not only defense against nature and animal but also against human predators, so organization for defensive and offensive action against other human groups is included here.

Adaptation to man's bio-social nature poses a second set of problems. A society cannot endure if it fails to meet the individual human needs of its members. In man these needs are not limited to food and clothing, but include psychic and cultural requirements which are not evident in anything like the same degree in animals. Social scientists have not been able to establish a list of highly *specific* individual needs which must be met by any society, nor can we say with certainty which common needs are rooted in man's biological inheritance and which are products of his long history of social living. There is general agreement, however, on the *types* of individual

[1] David F. Aberle, *et al.*, "The Functional Prerequisites of a Society," *Ethics* (1950), LX:100–111.

need which should be considered. These include the more obvious tissue needs for food and shelter, and the infinitely more complex need for sexual expression. Closely related, but not so well understood on the biological side, are needs for physical and psychic contact with other humans, for exercise, and for relaxation or release of tension. Still further from any specific physiological structure are expressive needs of the kinds usually manifested in dance, art, and probably in magic and war. Other needs, such as the need for status and self-respect, we cannot at all locate physiologically, but they are so nearly universal in social life that we must assume them to be rooted in man's basic bio-social human nature.

Without exception, every society takes special note of, and makes adjustments to, sex and age and biologically crucial events such as birth and death. Most societies also take account of individual temperamental differences, although less regularly and systematically. All provide special arrangements in the face of illness. Wherever there is social life, there is a distinctive pattern of leisure and recreation, some elaboration of crafts and art, and some form of religion expressed in a special set of ideas or myths and often in fairly elaborate ritual.

A number of plausible interpretations can be placed on these elaborations of human social life.[2] Certainly one important force generating these universal cultural forms is the need of the individual for certain satisfactions which go beyond his minimal requirements for food, shelter, and clothing. Such needs may be thought of as bio-social or psychic, and some adjustment to them must be made by every society.

Adaptation to the condition of collective living presents a third set of problems which every society must solve. Man could conceivably survive in his physical setting without social life. The need to satisfy his bio-social or psychic needs is probably what drives him to collective living. But finding himself living in groups, he is immediately confronted by a particular set of problems which go beyond the individual. Men living together must coordinate and integrate their actions to some degree to avoid chaos and confusion. In the collective life of animals and insects, this coordination is assured by instinct. In human society it is almost entirely a product of social invention. Man must elaborate rules and provide orderly procedures to determine who occupies given sites, to coordinate movement, to control the use of force and fraud, to regulate sexual behavior, to govern the conditions of exchange, and so on through the whole gamut of human relations. In the process of elaborating these rules, man creates the basic units of social organization. The invention of social organization was even more important than the invention of tools in setting man apart from the animal world.

The Units of Social Organization

Man is endlessly inventive. But his greatest invention is non-invention, the skill of transmitting intact and unchanged from one generation to the next the fundamental ways of doing things which he learned from the generation which preceded him. Children are conceived and reared, houses built, fish caught, and enemies killed in much the same way by most of the members of any society; and these patterns are maintained for relatively long periods of time. From the perspective of those in

[2] Clyde Kluckhohn, "Universal Values and Anthropological Relativism," *Modern Education and Human Values* (Pittsburgh: University of Pittsburgh Press, 1952), pp. 87–112, and "Universal Categories of Culture," in A. L. Kroeber (ed.), *Anthropology Today* (Chicago: University of Chicago Press, 1958), pp. 507–523.

each new generation, and for the society as an enduring, historical entity, this process of cultural transmission yields enormous economy. Thanks to it, each generation need not rediscover, at great cost in time and subject to great risk of failure, what those coming before have already learned. Not only is knowledge thus conserved, but the basis for communal life, resting on common information and understanding, is thus established. Since all those in each generation receive more or less the same cultural heritage from the preceding generation, they can more easily relate to one another and more effectively coordinate their actions.

The grand total of all the objects, ideas, knowledge, ways of doing things, habits, values, and attitudes which each generation in a society passes on to the next is what the anthropologist often refers to as the *culture* of a group. The transmission of culture is man's substitute for the instincts whereby most other living creatures are equipped with the means for coping with their environment and relating to one another. Yet it is more flexible than instinct, and can grow; that is, it can store new information, infinitely more rapidly than the process of mutation and biological evolution can enrich the instinctual storehouse of any other species.

From Folkways to Institutions

Custom, or alternatively, *folkways,* are the terms most commonly applied to the specialized and standardized ways of doing things common to those sharing a particular culture. The term can be applied to as small a social act [3] as a man's lifting his hat and saying "hello" on passing a woman he knows, or to as large and complex a set of events as the speeches, ceremonies, parades, and fireworks which grace the celebration of the Fourth of July in the United States. Custom, then, is any standardized and more or less specialized set of actions which is routinely carried out according to a generally accepted pattern in a given group. If the custom is not only routinely followed, but is, in addition, surrounded by sentiments or values such that failure to follow the expected pattern would produce strong sanctions from one's group, it is referred to as part of the *mores.* This distinction between folkways and mores lay at the heart of the work of the noted American sociologist William Graham Sumner.[4]

The association among customs is not random. Definite sets or complexes of customary ways of doing things, organized about a particular problem, or designed to attain a given objective, can be readily identified in any human community. Such a cluster of customary ways of doing things we designate a *role.* Roles are generally recognized and defined by the participants in a social system. They are, therefore, intimately tied to a set of expectations about which acts go with which others, in what sequence and under which conditions. Certain roles are open and can be assigned to anyone. A child asked to go out and rake the leaves has been temporarily assigned a role. He will be expected to follow a certain broadly defined sequence of acts, including putting the rake back in the garage when he is through. Any other child in the family might have been asked, and would have been expected to proceed in the same way.

Other roles are more highly specialized and become specific to particular individuals. When this degree of formalization exists, in particular when we use a specific name, title, or similar designation for certain role incum-

[3] The term social act is defined and discussed below in the section on social relationships, p. 71.

[4] William Graham Sumner, *Folkways* (Boston: Ginn, 1906), 692 pp.

bents, then a social *position* has been created. The term "status" is most commonly applied to such positions, but since this use of the term is easily confused with another, as in Vance Packard's *The Status Seekers*, as meaning prestige or standing in the community, we will speak either of "positions" or "status-positions." Within our family system we obviously do not recognize the status-position of "leaf-raker." In the occupational realm, however, where the degree of specialization is very much greater, we do recognize such rather narrowly defined positions as "stoker" on a coal ship or "fireman" on a train.

A *status-position*, then, is a socially recognized designation, a position in *social* as against geographical space, to which individuals may be assigned and which confers on the incumbent a set of rights and obligations. The rights and obligations constitute the role which the incumbent is expected to play. Positions may vary in the range and specificity of the roles they involve. In my status-position as rider on a public bus, my chief right is to be transported more or less directly to my destination. My obligations are largely limited to paying my fare, and not causing any disturbance to the other passengers. When I step into the position of husband or father, however, I acquire a large and complex set of roles involving a series of quite diffuse rights and obligations.

The paths of assignment to status-positions are generally distinguished on grounds of whether the position is ascribed or achieved. *Ascribed* status-positions are those to which individuals are more or less automatically assigned on the basis of accidents of birth. Age and sex form the most obvious bases for such ascription, and often color, caste, family line, and religion determine the assignment. *Achieved* status-positions are those in which a person is placed because of some action or attainment on his part. In our society political office and occupation or profession provide the most important examples of achieved positions, but one can treat the status-position of husband and wife in the same way. Certain achieved positions may be open only to those with prior qualifications on the basis of ascription, and many positions once open mainly to achievement are captured by a particular group and converted into ascribed positions.

Just as social acts may be aggregated into customs, and sets of such actions aggregated in roles, so a more complex structure of roles organized around some central activity or social need may be aggregated into an *institution*. E. B. Reuter, in his dictionary of sociological terms, proposes that we mean by institution: "The organized system of practices and social roles developed about a value or series of values,[5] and the machinery evolved to regulate the practices and administer the rules." [6]

Institutions lie at the center of sociological attention. They constitute the main building blocks of society. The number of institutions and the degree of their specialization vary from society to society. High civilizations and modern large-scale industrial societies are characterized by the intensive specialization of institutions organized around delimited problems of social life, and by the extensive internal elaboration of sub-systems within the larger institutions.

We must, therefore, think in terms of small-scale and large-scale institutions, and of complexes of institutions which form sub-systems within the larger society. At least four major sets or complexes of important institutions

[5] Values as a sociological term is defined and discussed below in this chapter, p. 74.
[6] Edward B. Reuter, *Handbook of Sociology* (New York: Dryden, 1941), p. 113.

are recognized by most sociologists. It will be evident, however, that each group could readily be broken up into several still categories.

First, are the *political institutions,* concerned with the exercise of power and which have a monopoly on the legitimate use of force. Institutions involving relations with other societies, including war, are also considered to fall into the political category. Second, there are the *economic institutions,* concerned with the production and distribution of goods and services. *Expressive-integrative* institutions, including those dealing with the arts, drama, and recreation, represent a third set. This group also includes institutions which deal with ideas, and with the transmission of received values. We may, therefore, include scientific, religious, philosophical, and educational organizations within this category. *Kinship institutions,* the fourth main category, are principally focused around the problem of regulating sex and providing a stable and secure framework for the care and rearing of the young.

Although it is helpful and to a degree accurate to think of institutions as organized mainly around *one* central problem of social existence, it is misleading to assume that each institution's contribution to social life is limited to that main concern. Each major institutional complex participates in and contributes in a number of ways to the life of the community. The family, for example, may be, and often is, itself a productive enterprise, and it always engages in the distribution of goods and services. Economic institutions not only produce goods and services but must have an internal order which involves the control of force and the exercise of legitimate authority. These considerations have led sociologists to make a distinction between social structures conceived of in either the analytic or the concrete sense. When speaking of *concrete structures,* they refer to the institutions we are all familiar with—families, courts, factories, and the like. By *analytic structures* they mean the whole set of social ways, spread over many concrete institutions, whereby a society manages to effect the production and distribution of goods, the control of force, and its other basic functional needs. For example, when we speak of "the structure of authority" in the analytic sense, we mean the way in which authority is organized and exercised not only in political affairs but also in the neighborhood, the church, the school, the family, and even in informal groups. Analytic structures are, therefore, constructs, products of the mind, abstracted from the concrete reality of a set of specific institutions.

A set of institutions constitutes a *social system,* of which the institutions may be thought of as sub-systems. The term "social system," like many others in sociology, is used to describe quite different levels of complexity. Thus, it is not uncommon to speak of the social system of a unit as small as a village or even a street-corner gang, and of those as large as a nation. Despite the ambiguity this introduces, it is at the present stage of our development a term without which we seem unable to manage.

Three elements are relevant to a definition of *community.* A community exists (1) when a set of households is relatively concentrated in a delimited geographical area; (2) their residents exhibit a substantial degree of integrated social interaction; and (3) have a sense of common membership, of belonging together, which is not based exclusively on ties of consanguinity. The example most commonly used, most familiar, and most directly accessible, is that of the peasant village. In such a village the peasants and their families usually live in fairly close proximity, and their common residence area is clearly demarcated and known to them. Most of the villagers' interaction is with other residents of the same village. The inhabitants will commonly consider themselves of the village, know its name, acknowledge their membership in the community, and be defined by and treated by those from other communities in accord with the standing of the village from which they come.

The *neighborhood* is simply a more limited form of community, but otherwise, it has the same characteristics. There is a physically distinctive territory, the inhabitants interact with one another relatively often, and they have a sense of belonging together. The neighborhood is usually the smallest residential unit, other than the household, recognized by sociology. The latter is not, customarily, spoken of as a community because it is predominantly organized on the basis of kinship.

As the size of a group inhabiting a given territory increases, there is an almost inevitable decrease in the probability of interaction between any two individuals chosen at random. When interaction between the average member and any other decreases beyond a certain point, the appropriateness of speaking of a community may be slight. In other words, physical proximity does not in itself make a community. A census tract arbitrarily and mechanically imposed on the map of a city does not bear any important relation to the more natural communities which develop in the different sections of a city. In what sense can the 10 million inhabitants of New York City be considered members of "a" community? In reply we might say that direct face-to-face interaction can be replaced to some degree by symbolic interaction, including that fostered by the media of mass communication. And a *sense* of common membership can be reinforced by external—i.e., legal or political—inducements to think of oneself as part of a specified community.

Although physical proximity does not automatically yield a community, can it exist at all in the absence of a common place of residence? This is basically the issue raised when we ask whether certain dispersed peoples, such as the Jews or the Armenians, constitute a "nation," since they do not inhabit a common territory. What we answer depends on our definition of community. If by a community we mean a group inhabiting a common area of residence, the answer is, by definition: "No." If, however, we define community mainly on the basis of frequency of interaction, or the feeling of common membership, the answer could be: "Yes." Certainly the idea that a community rests mainly on common feeling or belief is explicitly present in the expressions "a community of like-minded men" and "the world-wide community of scholars." Neither of these "communities" shares a specific and delimited area of residence.

The *essence* of community is a sense of common bond, the sharing of an identity, membership in a group holding some things, physical or spiritual, in common esteem, coupled with the acknowledgement of rights and obligations with reference to all others so identified. We may designate several types of community. A *residence community* (also called an ecological community) is one in which the bond which unites the members is common habitation of socially delineated physical space: a compound, neighborhood, town or village, city, region, or state. The term *moral or psychic community* is applied to those in which the sense of membership rests on a spiritual bond involving values, origins or belief. Either type may be largely *latent*, having merely a potential for common action, or *active*, with members interacting regularly and intensely. The natural small community of permanent residents such as a village, a town, or a neighborhood combines all these elements. It is an ecological and moral community, characteristically having a large number of realized interactions as well as a large number of latent bases for mobilizing a sense of solidarity in common membership.

Society: National and Worldwide

There is a type of social system larger than the institution and different from the community. Yet it is not automatically present whenever there is a set of institutions, nor does it automatically arise from every set of communities. It constitutes the largest unit with which sociology is ordinarily concerned, and is designated a *society*.

In *The Structure of Society* Marion Levy proposed 4 criteria which must be met by a group before it may be considered a society: The group must be capable of existing longer than the life span of the individual; it should recruit its new members at least in part by means of sexual reproduction; it should be united in giving allegiance to a common complex "general system of action"; and that system of action should be "self-sufficient." [7] The last of these criteria merits a few words of further explanation. By "system of action" we mean the total set of customs, values, and standard ways of acting which are commonly manifested by a group having relatively enduring mutual social relations. Systems of action may be relatively limited and moderately simple. For example, the relations between the teachers and pupils in a school represent the system of action specific to the school. We consider a system of action "self-sufficient" only if the rules, customs, and technology of a given group provide resources, knowledge, and legitimate power which normally arise in the course of social life.

According to this definition, the ordinary township in the United States, despite its high material culture and complex organization, would not be considered a society. It does not have the power to organize its own defense, and as a rule to deal with a murder it is obliged to rely on county or state police, courts, jails, and the like. A monastery would not qualify, even if its rules covered murder, because it makes no provision for sexual recruitment of new members. But these are essentially technical reservations. A simpler, although somewhat macabre, way to think about whether a group qualifies as a society would be to imagine that all other communities in the world except this one were suddenly to disappear. If there were a good chance that the surviving community would go forward in substantially its present form through subsequent generations, then it qualifies as a society. Most primitive tribes, however small, and virtually all nation states clearly meet this requirement. If a community could not survive under such a severe test, or could do so only by developing or elaborating many new institutional arrangements, such as a system of law and justice for which it formerly depended on a larger social system, then it does not qualify as a true society.

One can argue that the increased speed of travel, and the interlocking nature of world economy and international politics have, in effect, made a single, interacting community of all the people on earth. From this perspective one would maintain that there is a *worldwide social system*. Participation in this system is partly on an individual basis; partly on the basis of informal groups, as in the relations between relatives dispersed in different countries; and partly between more formally organized entities, such as companies doing business internationally, or international welfare organizations such as the Red Cross. The greatest portion of the interaction which characterizes the global social system, however, is accounted for by relations between the

[7] Marion Levy, *The Structure of Society* (Princeton: Princeton University Press, 1952), p. 113.

nation-states as units, or at least between individuals and groups acting as representatives or agents of such national units. These activities include diplomatic relations, the control of trade and movement, and war.

Whether the system of action in which the nations of the world participate constitutes a true worldwide *society*, in the sense in which we use the term, is certainly open to question. The issue hinges by our definition on the existence of a shared, self-sufficient system of action. On this test the world community seems seriously lacking. Very few values are shared by the majority of the world's people and fewer still are shared by their governments. Accepted mechanisms for the peaceful settlement of disputes, an indispensable element in any society, are poorly developed at the international level. The United Nations notwithstanding, there is no organized authority with the power to compel the nation-states' obedience to group decisions. We are today probably further from having a truly global society than the world knew under the hegemony of Rome or at the height of the power of the Church in medieval Europe. Yet there is reason to feel that since World War II we have come closer to developing a world society than was true at any point in the past few centuries.

The Nature of Social Relationships

In exploring the basic elements of social organization, we identified the institution, the community, and the society, each reflecting a different degree of completeness as a system of social action. But pursuing this line we neglected another set of distinctions which has an equally long and honorable place in sociology. One major mode of sociological analysis focuses mainly on the frequency and the qualities of *social relationships*. This approach can be applied to all the groups we have already discussed. It cuts across institutions, households, neighborhoods, community, and society.

The smallest unit to which sociological analysis is applied is "*the social act*." It has been written about at length by leading sociological thinkers such as Max Weber and George Herbert Mead,[8] but it remains an elusive concept and something difficult to measure. Most theorists apparently have in mind the smallest unit of directly visible action which has a reasonably clear shared meaning for both the actor and others with whom he is in contact. The instantaneous flick of the eyelid may serve as a simple example. If I merely "blink" spontaneously, especially as a reflex, the act is physical, but not social. But if I "wink," meaning to communicate the idea—"I am with you"—to someone I believe able to read the sign, then the movement of my eyelid is "a social act." If the other person responds by nodding or smiling, and he intends thereby to communicate receipt of the signal from me, then his nod is also "a social act." Taken together this sequence represents *a simple social interaction*. Social relationships may be conceived as made up of sets and patterns of such interaction sequences.

These ideas obviously invite numerous complications. We may ask, for example: Is an act social if I alone give it meaning? Is it social if it has no particular meaning for me, but has meaning for others? What about "internal" acts, which no one else can directly observe? Different, but equally

[8] Max Weber (A. Henderson and Talcott Parsons, trans.), *Theory of Economic and Social Organization* (New York: Oxford University Press, 1947), especially pp. 88–122; George Herbert Head (C. W. Morris, ed.), *Mind, Self and Society* (Chicago: University of Chicago Press, 1934), and (C. W. Morris, ed.), *The Philosophy of the Act* (Chicago: University of Chicago Press, 1950).

difficult, is the task of setting limits to the beginning and end of any social act. If I not only wink but also laugh and say, "Very funny," should each of these units be considered a social act, or only the entire sequence? It is obvious that challenging difficulties face those who aspire to classify and measure interaction in empirical research.

One can easily be tempted to see in the sociological concepts of "the act" and "the relationship" an analogy with the atom and the molecule in physics and with the cell and tissue in biology. These are the basic units of which are built all the larger and more complex structures relevant to the respective disciplines. It will be no surprise, therefore, that many leading sociological theorists sought to develop a set of terms to distinguish different types of relationship and to increase our understanding of them. Sociological writing is replete with schemes for classifying social relationships, varying greatly in complexity, sophistication, and thoroughness. Perhaps the most honored is Charles Cooley's distinction between primary and secondary relationships.[9] A primary relationship, according to Cooley, is one in which intimate face-to-face association and cooperation predominate, as a result of which individuals become fused into a common whole epitomized by stress on "we" rather than "I." Similar, and equally well-known distinctions, were elaborated by Tönnies in Germany [10] and by Durkheim in France.[11]

Not only have these distinctions endured, but so have the difficulties of using the concepts with any degree of precision. As Kingsley Davis has pointed out, Cooley's stress on "we" feeling cannot be taken as the distinctive element in a primary group since this same feeling is to some degree necessary for any enduring community. It must exist even in the great nations, in which there clearly can be face-to-face contact between only a small proportion of the members.[12]

The obvious difficulty is that concepts such as Cooley's primary group and Tönnies' *gemeinschaft* assume the factual coherence of a set of discrete aspects of relationships which may or may not combine in reality as the sociologist thought they would. Such concepts, are, in other words, rather global summaries; they refer to the hypothetical rather than to the empirically demonstrated. One of the tasks of those following Cooley and Tönnies, therefore, has been to designate more precisely what are the aspects of any relationship. The underlying justification for these efforts at conceptual clarification is, of course, the hope that more precise conceptual distinctions will encourage more exact observation and measurement. The accumulation of data based on direct observation would enable us more accurately to describe the actual pattern of association between various dimensions of interaction which is *assumed* to exist when we use concepts such as "the primary group."

One distinction we obviously must make in describing any relationship is that between quantitative and qualitative aspects. The quantitative elements include, first and foremost, the number of people participating in the system of action, their concentration or dispersion in geographical space, the frequency with which they interact with one another, and the relative duration of their association.

[9] Charles H. Cooley, *Human Nature and the Social Order* (New York: Scribner, 1902).

[10] Ferdinand Tönnies (C. P. Loomis, trans.), *Fundamental Concepts of Sociology* (New York: American Book, 1940).

[11] Émile Durkheim (G. Simpson, trans.), *The Division of Labor in Society* (Glencoe, Ill.: The Free Press, 1949). These terms are defined in Chap. 3.

[12] Kingsley Davis, *Human Society* (New York: Macmillan, 1957), p. 303.

The qualitative aspects of the interaction are less easy to agree about. Kingsley Davis distinguishes 5 characteristics which, when combined with certain information concerning the quantitative aspect (which he calls "physical conditions") serve him as a basis for discriminating primary from secondary relationships.[13] He gives examples of these at the level of both the dyad and the larger group. His scheme is given in Table 2.

[13] *Ibid.*, pp. 294–298.

Table 2

Primary and Secondary Relationships *

Primary

Physical Conditions	*Social Characteristics*	*Sample Relationships*	*Sample Groups*
Spatial proximity	Identification of ends	Friend-friend	Play group
Small number	Intrinsic valuation of the relation	Husband-wife	Family
Long duration	Intrinsic valuation of other person	Parent-child	Village or neighborhood
	Inclusive knowledge of other person	Teacher-pupil	Work-team
	Feeling of freedom and spontaneity		
	Operation of informal controls		

Secondary

Physical Conditions	*Social Characteristics*	*Sample Relationships*	*Sample Groups*
Spatial distance	Disparity of ends	Clerk-customer	Nation
Large number	Extrinsic valuation of the relation	Announcer-listener	Clerical
Short duration	Extrinsic valuation of other person	Performer-spectator	Professional association
	Specialized and limited knowledge of other person	Officer-subordinate	Corporation
	Feeling of external constraint	Author-reader	
	Operation of formal controls		

* Kingsley Davis, *Human Society* (New York: Macmillan, 1957), p. 306.

Professor Davis' scheme is a variant on one more widely known, developed by Talcott Parsons.[14] He uses a set of 5 "pattern variables" to distinguish the aspects of any social relationship. According to Parsons, each time we act, and in each role in which we act, we are, in effect, emphasizing one or another side of the 5 basic divisions. If a role is *specific*, our relationship is limited to one particular narrowly defined exchange; if it is *diffuse*, our involvement will extend over a wide variety of problems or relationships. We stress either *affectivity* (that is, feeling, emotion, and gratification), or *affective neutrality*, which means we place more emphasis on instrumental or moral considerations. We manifest *particularism* when we give special consideration to people because of their relationship to us, whereas if we evidence *universalism*, we treat more or less alike all who come before us in a given status-position. If my treatment of you is mainly on the basis of what you are in yourself, in contrast to what you do or have done, I stress *quality* over *performance*. When my concern is mainly to advance the goals of the group, I display a *collectivity-orientation*, whereas if I am most concerned to advance my own interests through our relationship, I stress *self-orientation*. Described in these terms, the relations of husband and wife, and indeed all nuclear family relations, tend to be diffuse, affective, and particularistic, and reflect stress on quality and collectivity-orientation. The relationship between a clerk and a customer would be at the opposite pole on each dimension.

Precision in the delineation of concepts is a necessary, although not sufficient, condition for exact empirical observation. After decades of talk about the components of interaction within groups, it was only after World War II that we began systematically to measure precisely the content of group interaction. Among the most notable of these efforts is the work of Professor Robert Bales in the Laboratory of Social Relations at Harvard.[15] Professor Bales' technique, called Interaction Process Analysis is sufficiently advanced so that by study of a discussion group's interaction "profile" one can tell at a glance whether it is a dissatisfied group or one with high morale. I have given an example of such profiles in Table 5, Chapter 7.

The Study of Values

Although the most dramatic advances in the direct observation of interpersonal relations and the measurement of interaction have been made in the laboratory, significant progress is also being made in studying relationships in real life. These studies, however, more often deal with *values* about human relations rather than with behavior directly observed.

The term "values" has almost as much importance in sociology as the terms "institution" and "social system." Individuals, groups, organizations, societies, and cultures are all spoken of as "having," "expressing," and "pursuing" values. Like many another sociological term, "values" carries a heavy load indeed. In the many definitions of values proposed by sociologists and anthropologists, the common element lies in the recognition of values as an expression of the ultimate ends, goals, or purposes of social action. Values deal not so much with what is, but with what ought to be; in other words, they express moral imperatives. Thus, when Weber identified the importance to Benjamin Franklin of sobriety, strict ethics in business relations, and the avoidance of indulgence, he was describing Franklin's values. Almost any conceivable aspect of any relationship can be, and somewhere probably has

[14] Talcott Parsons, *The Social System* (Glencoe, Ill.: The Free Press, 1951).
[15] See also Chaps. 3 and 7.

been, made an object of value. Honesty and duplicity, silence and loquaciousness, stoicism and emotionality, restless activity and passive acceptance, all have been deeply valued in different societies.

Much the same range of human qualities and aspects of relationships are recognized in most societies, the main differences between cultures being in the value they put on these qualities as important or minor, good or bad. One values aggressiveness and deplores passivity, another the reverse. And a third gives little attention to this dimension altogether, emphasizing instead the virtue of sobriety over emotionality, which may be quite unimportant in either of the other cultures.[16]

As was true in the study of interactions, it was only after World War II that social scientists went beyond merely defining and discussing values and began actively to measure their nature and distribution. One of the most complex and interesting of these efforts has been carried out by Florence Kluckhohn. She began by defining certain basic "common human problems for which all peoples, at all times must find some solution." [17] All societies, she maintained adopt some value position with regard to man's relation to other men, to nature, to time, and to activity. She argued that all cultures had discovered pretty much the same range of positions or alternatives one might take with regard to these life problems, but that different cultures placed different *value* on the various alternatives.

To establish her point Dr. Kluckhohn studied 5 small communities, each with an apparently distinctive way of life but all inhabiting the same area in the American Southwest. The groups included a Mormon settlement, one of ex-Texans, a village of Spanish-Americans, and both Zuñi and Navaho Indian reservations. To samples from each community she presented the same set of basic human situations, and recorded the alternative solutions they preferred. She found that the groups were indeed different, and "no two of the cultures chose exactly the same pattern of preferences on any of the (value) orientations." [18]

The two English-speaking groups were most alike, although differing in important respects. They seemed to represent one pole, the Spanish-Americans the other, with the Indian groups falling somewhere between. For example, the Texans were more individualistic rather than concerned with the extended family group, were oriented to the future rather than to the past, inclined to see man as over nature rather than as subjugated to it, and on the activity dimension were predominantly interested in "doing." By contrast, the Spanish-Americans stressed lineality (the principle which sees the individual mainly in terms of his relation to an ordered succession of social positions enduring through time); they were more oriented to the present than to the future; they viewed man as subjugated to nature; and they strongly preferred "being" over "doing." [19]

Public-opinion surveys, especially those more recently conducted on an international scale, also permit us to speak more authoritatively about the distribution of values in larger groups up to the size of nations. For example, in 1958 adults in 11 countries were asked what they thought it most important to teach children. Some of the results are summarized in Table 3.

[16] For one general reference see Charles Osgood, *The Measurement of Meaning* (Urbana: University of Illinois Press, 1957).

[17] Florence Kluckhohn and Fred L. Strodtbeck, *Variation in Value Orientation* (New York: Harper & Row, 1961), p. 10.

[18] *Ibid.*, p. 172.

[19] *Ibid.*, p. 170 *ff*.

Table 3

Values in Child-rearing, in Percentages by Country and Socio-economic Status *

Country and Child-rearing Values	*Upper*	*Socio-economic Status Middle*	*Lower*
Australia			
Ambition	5	3	8
Obedience to parents	13	17	23
Enjoyment	..	..	1
Trust in God	26	33	25
Decency; honesty	60	51	45
Don't know	5	4	3
No. of respondents	94	313	367
Denmark			
Ambition	11	13	9
Obedience to parents	14	18	15
Enjoyment	2	1	3
Trust in God	16	9	10
Decency; honesty	54	56	61
Don't know	3	3	2
No. of respondents	167	390	129
Japan			
Ambition	20	24	22
Obedience to parents	6	9	19
Enjoyment	4	3	1
Trust in God	4	4	6
Decency; honesty	64	58	46
Don't know	2	2	6
No. of respondents	368	422	69
Netherlands			
Ambition	8	4	3
Obedience to parents	4	9	12
Enjoyment	1	2	2
Trust in God	40	41	37
Decency; honesty	46	48	50
Don't know	4	2	2
No. of respondents	214	147	142

* Data provided by International Research Associates, from a release of March 13, 1958. Since some respondents insisted that two values were equally important, the answers for several countries total more than 100%.

Alex Inkeles, "Industrial Man: The Relation of Status to Experience, Perception and Value," *American Journal of Sociology* (January 1960), 66:224.

In all of the countries, and at all economic levels, decency and honesty were the most important values, generally chosen by about half of those interviewed. This suggests that some values are equally important to all people, and provides a basis for assuming the existence of a set of pan-human values. But there are also great differences in the relative importance of other values in the several countries. Ambition is clearly the second most important values in all classes in Japan, whereas it is of very minor importance in Australia and the Netherlands. Correspondingly, "trust in God" is quite heavily emphasized in Denmark and Australia, but to the Japanese it seems hardly worth mentioning as a quality to inculcate in children.

The greatly improved techniques we have developed for the direct observation and recording of human interaction, and the impressive strides we are now able to make in studying values about interpersonal relations held by groups as large as national populations, suggest that in coming decades those who view sociology as mainly the study of social relationships may, through the quality of their research, win many new adherents to their point of view.

six

fundamental social processes

If sociology went no further than to offer an elaborate set of concepts referring to community and society, status and role, primary and secondary groups, folkways and custom, it would still contribute to our thinking about man in society. It would also present an extremely static conception, analogous to anatomy without physiology. The processes, the flows and exchanges of action and reaction, with which sociology concerns itself are numerous. Dealing with them is complicated by the fact that essentially the same process has often been designated by quite different labels, each having widespread currency. We cannot, therefore, hope to be exhaustive in this presentation. But a brief discussion of conformity and deviance, stratification, and social change should serve to introduce the more important social processes and to impart some sense of how sociology approaches them.

Our discussion of these 3 processes must serve to represent a much larger set of processes which characterize all social systems, but which we could take up fully only if this were an exhaustive treatise rather than a modest introduction to sociology. Competition and cooperation, conflict and accommodation, immigration and assimilation, integration and segregation, concentration and dispersion, imitation and diffusion—these terms suggest the range and complexity of the processes which we might discuss. The list is large, but by no means endless. Sociological interests vary with the times. Some processes once given a great deal of attention, such as imitation, no longer capture the sociological imagination. Whatever the process, however, its significance lies not in itself, but in its contribution to the flow of social life.

Conformity, Variation, and Deviance

The social order depends on the regular and adequate fulfillment of the role obligations incurred by the incumbents of the major status-positions in a social system. It follows that the most important process in society is that which insures that people do indeed meet their role obligations. The processes of conformity, variation, and deviance are, therefore, among the most crucial with which sociology concerns itself.

Most people assume, almost glibly, that they know the meaning of conformity. It means doing what you are supposed to do, as exemplified by the child who puts on his rubbers when his mother tells him to, the pupil who does his homework assignment, the motorist who stops his car at the intersection until the policeman signals that he may proceed, and the citizen who honestly pays his taxes. In all these examples the status-position is clear-cut, the behavior required explicit and limited, the rules unambiguous, and the power to enforce conformity physically embodied and close at hand. Sociology starts here with what we all know and accept; conformity to role obligations rests in good part on *sanctions:* the power of others—individuals, groups, and the community—to enforce their expectations by the use of reward and punishment.

The ultimate negative sanction is, of course, death. Negative sanctions range through all forms of physical force down to mild restraint. They include, as well, psychological punishments from the most degrading public humiliation, through ridicule, to mild forms of censure such as are implicit in many nominally friendly jibes and critical jokes. Negative sanctions may be effected not only in doing, but in not doing. In our psychological-minded era, everyone has become familiar with the idea of the "withholding of love" as a sanction parents apply to control their children.

There is an obvious difficulty in relying on sanctions to insure conformity to crucial role obligations: Someone must always be around to observe what happens and to dispense rewards and punishment. Although we are all to some extent our brothers' keepers, no society could manage even a small part of its diverse tasks if conformity to role obligation rested solely on such ubiquitous supervision. *Motivation,* the readiness and desire of the individual to fulfill his role obligations is, therefore, an indispensable underpinning which supports the network of roles and insures the reasonably smooth flow of social activity without excessive social investment in supervision by others. Finally, neither sanctions nor motivation to perform can be successful where the incumbent of status-position does not understand clearly what is required of him.

When an individual has incorporated within himself knowledge and appropriate skills necessary to the fulfillment of a role, and when he accepts the value or appropriateness of the action, sociologists speak of his having "internalized" the role and its psychological underpinnings. The term *socialization* is used to describe the process whereby individuals learn their culture, both in its most general form and as it applies to particular roles. Although it usually refers to the learning of children, the term socialization may be used in exactly the same sense to describe adults learning what is required of them in a new job or some other status-position which they are entering.

A complaint long directed against anthropologists, and sometimes made with equal justice about sociologists, is that they too readily assume that the members of society hold the same values and beliefs and share a common pattern of action. In trying to develop a "model" of any society, the social scientist almost inevitably gives us a simplified picture which gravely understates the variety and diversity of attitude and behavior found in most societies. Cultural norms and ways of doing things seldom involve rigid and uniform requirements. They usually permit a fairly wide range in the way things are done. We are expected to cross streets at the crossing, but people cross them at all places and in all ways without, in most cases, very much being made of the fact. Even with regard to the most fundamental issues of life, most cultures do not hold a single unified set of beliefs. Rather, they harbor both dominant and quite acceptable variant values.[1] Most Americans are either present or future oriented, but it is quite acceptable to look to and value the past. Indeed, some social groups in some sections of the country, notably New England and the South, rest their social distinction in part on their preoccupation with the past.

Deviance, then, is not necessarily inherent in every departure from a commonly accepted standard, nor in holding any minority view. This would be statistical deviance, but not social deviance. *Social deviance* arises when the departure from accepted norms involves action about which the community feels strongly, so strongly as to adopt sanctions to prevent or otherwise control the deviant behavior. In other words, deviant behavior is not merely oblique to dominant or "core" values, but is antithetical to them. The point is clear-cut in the case of major crimes. But the issue can also become clouded, and the designation "deviant" very ambiguous. Exceeding the speed limit on the highway is against the law. Is it still deviance if almost everyone does it? In Mississippi local citizens engaged in armed resistance to United States marshals trying to carry out an order of a Federal Court instructing them to effect the enrollment of a Negro in the University of Mississippi. The local grand jury in Mississippi wished to send the marshals, not the rioters, to jail. Obviously, what is deviant may be different from the perspective of different groups participating in the same larger system of action. Landlords owning property near crowded army camps may, for substandard housing, charge the dependents of mobilized soldiers much higher rents than those commonly collected in their region. Are they merely following the accepted business practice in taking advantage of an opportunity for profit, or is their action a deviation from moral norms?

In the United States the study of social deviance has been largely limited to the study of certain social problems such as crime, juvenile delinquency, prostitution, drug addiction, and the like, all of which are most common among the lower classes, and in the more depressed and disadvantaged segments of modern industrial society. In the development of such studies a major role was played by the sociologists at the University of Chicago, whose home city provided a great natural laboratory for the pursuit of such investigations. The guiding idea and connecting thread in these studies was the conviction that such deviations from accepted social norms were not a product of mental deficiency, of psychosis, or other forms of personal and psychic aberration, but rather had social roots and were caused by social conditions. Chief among these were the neglect and consequent deteriora-

[1] Florence Kluckhohn and Fred L. Strodtbeck, *Variations in Value Orientations* (New York: Harper & Row, 1961). The terms of dominant and variant values have been proposed by Florence Kluckhohn. Her comparative study of values in the American Southwest, described in Chap. 5, gives ample evidence for the point made here.

tion of certain parts of the city, which produced social disorganization and in turn bred deviant behavior of all kinds.

One of the typical, and most important, of this series of investigations was that by Clifford Shaw and his associates on juvenile delinquency.[2] By dividing the city into mile-square areas and recording for each the proportion of delinquent boys, they were able to demonstrate dramatically that delinquents came overwhelmingly from a small number of areas around the central business district, or "Loop," along the Chicago River, near the stockyards, and in the vicinity of the steel mills in South Chicago.[3] In some of these mile-square areas as many as one fourth of all the boys were entered on the police blotter at least once in the course of a year, whereas in the great majority of districts 1 per cent or less were so entered. The high delinquency areas, although physically separated, were all areas of transition, being invaded by industry and business, with declining populations living in conditions of physical deterioration and experiencing the culture conflict attendant on rapid change.

From these considerations Shaw and his associates drew a conclusion about delinquency striking similar to that developed much earlier by Durkheim to explain suicide. They reasoned that under the conditions existing in slum districts the community becomes disorganized, and its hold on its members weakened to the point where individuals are not constrained to follow the social norms. In their words: "If the community is disorganized and weak in its control, it will be easy for institutions to disintegrate and behavior will not be controlled by conventional standards." [4] Furthermore, they argued that under these conditions criminal patterns are so common, and are transmitted so freely, that they become, in fact, the dominant culture in high-delinquency areas. Young boys and girls growing up in these districts, therefore, spontaneously come to learn and accept delinquent patterns as the natural way of behaving.

The work of Shaw and his associates certainly presented a sharp sociological challenge to the then current ideas about delinquency as mainly a product of mentally defective or inherently vicious boys who were somehow nature's accidents. But it has itself been since seriously challenged by subsequent work. Perhaps most important was the research of the Gluecks at Harvard, who showed decisively that the transitional zone alone could not explain delinquency since within those zones only some boys, generally a minority, acted in a delinquent way.[5]

The Gluecks compared 500 persistent delinquents with 500 non-delinquent boys living in the same district and of comparable age, intelligence, and ethnic origin. Their findings supported Shaw's conclusion that psychological difficulties such as psychopathy or neuroticism could not explain the differences between the two groups, nor could differences in physical strength or the like. They did find, however, that the delinquent boys much more often came from families which often moved, in which only one parent was present, the father had bad work habits, alcoholism was prevalent, and so on through a host of disadvantages. It was, therefore, clear that although the delinquent culture existed throughout the district, it affected only those

[2] Clifford Shaw, *et al.*, *Delinquency Areas* (Chicago: University of Chicago Press, 1929), 214 pp.

[3] *Ibid.*, p. 203.

[4] *Ibid.*, p. 6.

[5] Sheldon Glueck and Eleanor Glueck, *Unraveling Juvenile Delinquency* (Cambridge: Harvard University Press, 1955).

boys with certain prior family experiences which apparently predisposed them to delinquency either by affecting their character or by leaving them inadequately supervised, or both.

Quite a different challenge to the earlier thinking about delinquency is posed by the recent work of Richard Cloward and Lloyd Ohlin.[6] Most students of the problem assume that delinquent boys have *rejected* the dominant middle-class values of society. Cloward and Ohlin believe that lower-class delinquent boys have the same values as those in the middle class, but finding legitimate paths for attaining those goals blocked, they turn instead to illegitimate means. While the Shaw approach would suggest urban renewal and the Gluecks' family rehabilitation, the solution obviously following from the Cloward and Ohlin theory is to provide lower-class boys with more legitimate opportunities to attain middle-class goals. This idea is reflected in the title of their book—*Delinquency and Opportunity*. It has become the basis for a large-scale experimental program of action-research in New York City designed to test the efficacy of this idea.

Although American sociology of the Chicago school made major contributions to our understanding of deviant behavior through its work on problems such as delinquency, it nevertheless seemed to define deviance as if it were exclusively a characteristic of the more disadvantaged classes of society. Edwin H. Sutherland began a long overdue revolution in the American study of deviant behavior in a pioneering paper on "White Collar Criminality" which he published in 1940.[7] He drew together a variety of striking bits of evidence which indicated how widespread, indeed ubiquitous, were violations of criminal law statutes on the part of "men of affairs, of experience, of refinement and culture, of excellent reputation and standing." Among the crimes he discussed were embezzlement, fraud, bribery, misapplication of funds, false grading and weights, and violations of a number of federal regulatory statutes such as the Sherman Antitrust Act and the Pure Food and Drugs Law.

Sutherland rejected the argument that such cases referred merely to standard sharp business practice. He argued that even though it is not ordinarily called crime: "White collar crime is real crime . . . because it is in violation of the criminal law (and belongs within the scope of criminology). The crucial question . . . is the criterion of violation of the criminal law." [8] Not only on this technical ground, but also because white-collar crime is so expensive to society and so deleterious in its effect on social trust and confidence, Sutherland urged that criminologists seriously study it as intensively as they had been studying crimes such as assault, burglary and robbery, larceny, and the sex offenses more prevalent in the lower classes.

The campaign so vigorously begun by Sutherland in 1940 mirrored a more widespread dissatisfaction with the narrow definition of deviant behavior prevalent in American sociology. The broader perspective which is coming to replace it is reflected in the fact that the most popular and prestigious introduction to the field of deviance available during the 1960's contained chapters not only on the usual themes of crime and prostitution,

[6] Richard Cloward and Lloyd Ohlin, *Delinquency and Opportunity* (Glencoe, Ill.: The Free Press, 1961).

[7] Edwin Sutherland, "White-collar Criminality," *American Sociological Review* (1940), V:1–12. See also Albert Cohen, *et al.* (eds.), *The Sutherland Papers* (Bloomington: Indiana University Press, 1956).

[8] Sutherland, *American Sociological Review* (1940), V:5.

but also on the world of work, on traffic and transportation in the metropolis, and on race and ethnic relations. Deviant political and religious behavior still were not systematically dealt with, however, and as Robert Merton, the book's editor, acknowledged, we are still far from attaining a single, overarching or comprehensive, theory of deviant behavior.[9]

Stratification and Mobility

There is no society known which does not make some distinction between individuals by ranking them on some scale of value.[10] The most ubiquitous is that between men and women. But such distinctions may rest on almost any basis, involving either ascribed or achieved status. Even in the societies with the simplest technology, the good hunter is distinguished from the poorer one and is generally accorded prestige or higher standing in the community. The more complex the technology, the greater the specialization, the more extensive the degree of social differentiation, the more bases are established for differential valuation.

Such prestige rankings are often referred to as status rankings. It is that sense of the word that almost everyone has come to know of "The Status Seekers." Many radical religious and political philosophies treat all such distinctions as invidious, and indeed evil. They urge the establishment of a world in which these distinctions no longer exist, and instead all men are *valued* as equal. Most sociologists are dubious of the possibility of creating such a society, and the unhappy fate of most utopian communities makes this skepticism warranted. There is good reason to assume that ranking people is inherent in man, and that no society will ever be without it.

Differential valuation is unfortunately commonly confused with differential possessions, such as skill, power, or economic resources. Sociologists insist on keeping these categories quite distinct. Exploring the actual relation between differential possessions and differential prestige is one of the more important and interesting tasks the sociologist can find. The interrelations are by no means obvious or simple. Prestige may be used to win access to economic advantage, and both power and money may be used to buy standing in the community—or at least the outward evidences of respect and prestige.

The individuals in any society may be placed on a scale or hierarchy of value expressing the prestige or respect in which each person is held. Those sharing more or less comparable standing will then form a *prestige group*, or stratum. In some societies these arrangements are formal and explicit. They may be religiously sanctioned, as in the Indian caste system, and even enforced by law. Similarly, individuals may be placed on a scale of possessions, separately for political power, land, and money. Those having similar shares of power or wealth can be grouped and considered as forming a stratum, or *class*, in the hierarchy of possessions.

When we speak of the stratification system in any society we refer to the nature of its hierarchies of possessions and status, the bases for assignment to positions in these hierarchies, and to the relations between the two hierarchies and among groups within each hierarchy. No problem in sociology has received more attention in the last 3 decades, and probably no

[9] Robert K. Merton and Robert A. Nisbet (eds.), *Contemporary Social Problems* (New York: Harcourt, Brace & World, 1961).

[10] See the section on values in the preceding chapter.

other has been the subject of more confusion. This attention stems in good part not only from the basic importance of the issues but also from the special role which the theory of stratification plays in the Marxist scheme.

The sociological attack on the problem of stratification seeks to answer a series of questions. The first is: What is the structure of stratification in any given society or group? The task here is mainly descriptive, a job of social mapping. The sociologist tries to determine how many classes there are, what their characteristics are in terms of income, occupation, and prestige, how large each class is, where its members are located in physical and social space, and so on.

The task of description proves more difficult than it might seem on first glance, because it rests on decisions about a second issue: What should be the basis for measuring stratification? There are two main competing approaches adopted in placing people in social strata. The "objective" measures assign great weight to the amount of income, or to possessions, education, or power a man has. The more "subjective," or psychological, measures rely more on the *feelings* a man has about which class he belongs in, or depend on the *opinion* which others have about where they would place a given person in the class hierarchy.

If more than one index of class position is to be allowed, this immediately raises serious questions about a third issue: What are the interrelations between the different measures? Accepting the principle of assignment on the basis of multiple indicators forces us to inquire into the degree of association among the indicators. If the indicators agree, there is no great problem. There clearly is a distinct class if those at the top in education, income, power, and possession are all the same set of men. This was essentially the condition Lloyd Warner found in his famous study of "Yankee City" during the 'thirties.[11]

Warner and his associates placed every one living in an old industrial port city of some 17,000 people in 1 of 6 classes on the basis of reputation or social standing. They then studied other aspects of the life of each class, and found these strongly associated with standing in the hierarchy of social position. Of those classified as belonging to the upper-upper class, 84 per cent were, by occupation, proprietors or professionals. The remainder were in clerical or kindred occupations and none was tainted by connections with wholesale and retail business or industrial labor.[12] Ninety per cent of those in the upper class who were "employable" had jobs, whereas in the lower-lower class in that period of depression only 26 per cent were fully employed.[13] In keeping with their occupational status, the upper-uppers enjoyed the highest incomes, with an average of $6,400 coming into each of their families as contrasted with $882 per family in the lower-lower class.[14] The upper-upper families almost invariably lived in the best districts of town, and in large and better quality homes. The median value of the real estate they owned was more than $5,800, whereas among owners in the lower-lower class it was $1,600.[15] The advantages of the upper classes also extended into the realm of political power. They held twice as many political posts as their

[11] W. Lloyd Warner and Paul A. Lunt, *The Social Life of a Modern Community* (New Haven: Yale University Press, 1941).

[12] *Ibid.*, p. 261.

[13] *Ibid.*, p. 424.

[14] *Ibid.*, p. 290.

[15] *Ibid.*, p. 282.

proportion of the city population. More important, they were concentrated in the relatively more powerful public offices. Although they did not have a monopoly of political power, it could be said that "the upper classes, together with the upper-middle class, dominate the high control offices" in Yankee City.[16]

Since the leading stratum in Yankee City stood at the top on all the relevant hierarchies, there is little reason to challenge the assertion that they represented a distinctive social class. Indeed, we may acknowledge the existence of social classes even when groups do not have a homogeneous set of rankings so long as they are consistently placed in certain positions. In other words, we may still speak of classes if those with the most power prove *consistently* to be in the middle range of incomes yet *consistently* fall in the low range of education. But what if the men of power include in their ranks men of both high and low income, and some high and some low in education and in standing in the community? This condition has been demonstrated to exist in a number of American communities, and has been particularly well documented in an outstanding study of New Haven conducted by Robert Dahl.[17] Even in Yankee City, as we noted, the upper classes had to share power with the middle classes. And the other classes were by no means so consistently homogeneous as was the upper-upper. In the lower-middle class, for example, all types of occupation were strongly represented, ranging from the professional and proprietary (14 per cent) to the semi-skilled worker (27 per cent).[18] About as many lived in large and medium-size houses in good repair as lived in small houses in poor physical condition.[19] In the face of such diversity within one group, can we still sensibly speak of it as a social class?

Our response depends on the answer to still a fourth question: What are the relations between any set of men who share some common position on one or more indicators of class? Some sociologists argue that a class is constituted only when men have a common outlook, and in particular, only when they regularly meet together, have social intercourse, or act together to advance their common interest. It is largely in this latter sense that C. W. Mills argued that the United States is governed by a "power-elite" of generals and businessmen which makes all the really important decisions affecting our lives.[20]

It is, of course, much easier to make such assertions than to prove them. Although Mills presents some material concerning overlapping membership in major corporations and government service, it remains unclear how much of a monopoly of power these associations have, and how far they act in concert or in competition with each other. On a number of these points Mills has been challenged rather effectively by Daniel Bell, who argues the case for a series of more or less independent and competing elites.[21] Decisions at the national level are harder to trace precisely than those at the local. Floyd Hunter, who studied community leadership in Atlanta, reached the conclusion that there was indeed a power elite of men who were in intimate

[16] *Ibid.*, p. 372.

[17] Robert Dahl, *Who Governs? Democracy and Power in an American City* (New Haven: Yale University Press, 1962).

[18] Warner and Lunt, *The Social Life of a Modern Community*, p. 261.

[19] *Ibid.*, p. 245.

[20] C. Wright Mills, *The Power Elite* (New York: Oxford University Press, 1957).

[21] Daniel Bell, "Is There a Ruling Class in America?", *The End of Ideology* (Glencoe, Ill.: The Free Press, 1960), pp. 43–67.

contact and represented a clique without whose initiative or approval no important community action could be undertaken.[22] But Hunter based his investigation mainly on the reputation of the leaders rather than by directly reviewing the history of a series of proposals or decisions. Studies which have adopted this more systematic approach, such as Dahl's in New Haven, cast serious doubt on Hunter's assumption about the existence of a single, cohesive power elite in the typical American city.

Elites, and indeed any other stratum, may be stable and even permanent, or they may experience rapid and extensive turnover. A man moving from one job to another, but at much the same level of prestige or income, is engaged in horizontal mobility. This type arouses little interest among sociologists. Movement from one stratum to another up or down any one of the possible stratification hierarchies is called *vertical mobility*. This type of movement suggests a fifth question to which students of this field avidly address themselves: What are the rates of social mobility?

Rates of social mobility may be computed either within the life span of a man or, as is more common, between generations of fathers and sons. Sociologists long entertained the belief, without too systematically examining the data, that certain societies, such as India, had highly *closed systems of stratification*—that is, there was little upward mobility and almost all sons ended up in precisely the same stratum their fathers had occupied. This type of stratification is contrasted with relatively *open-class systems*, such as that in the United States, which was long assumed to have a distinctively high rate of upward mobility.

Recent investigations have taught us to be more cautious about accepting such traditional, essentially stereotyped images.[23] A study of inter-generational mobility in 18 countries shows that frequent movement by the sons of manual workers into white-collar jobs is much more common and widespread than had been believed.[24] In some underdeveloped countries, such as Italy and Puerto Rico, only about 10 to 15 per cent of the sons of men who worked with their hands attained white-collar positions. But in 9 of the 18 countries the rate was much higher, ranging between 24 and 31 per cent. The United States did not have a distinctive rate, but rather shared its leading position with several other countries. Even India, always held up as the leading example of a society with a rigidly fixed caste system, reported a mobility rate of 27 per cent, although this was limited to an urban sample from industrial Poona. Perhaps even more striking was the evidence concerning the formerly neglected subject of downward mobility. In many countries movement down into the manual class by sons of fathers with white-collar positions is as common as is upward mobility. Indeed, in 3 countries, the Netherlands, Puerto Rico, and Great Britain, more than 40 per cent of the sons of white-collar fathers become manual, usually industrial, workers.[25]

However elites may secure their position, whether by inheritance, through talent, or by force, many feel the most important question of all to be the sixth: What is the influence of the class structure on the lives of the class

[22] Floyd Hunter, *Community Power Structure: A Study of Decision Makers* (Chapel Hill: University of North Carolina Press, 1953).

[23] A pioneering role in challenging these ideas was played by S. Martin Lipset and Reinhard Bendix, *Social Mobility in Industrial Society* (Berkeley: University of California Press, 1959).

[24] S. M. Miller, "Comparative Social Mobility," *Current Sociology* (1960), IX:1–89.

[25] *Ibid.*, p. 34.

Table 4

The Relation of Democratic Government to Indices of Wealth, Industrialization, Education and Urbanization *

Countries in:	*Per-capita Income (dollars)*	*Percentage of Males in Agriculture*	*Number in School beyond Primary Grades (per 1,000 pop.)*	*Percentage in Metropolitan Areas*
Europe				
More democratic	695	21	44	38
Less democratic	308	41	22	23
Latin America				
More democratic	171	52	13	26
Less democratic	119	67	8	15

* Adapted from S. Martin Lipset, *Political Man* (New York: Doubleday, 1960), pp. 51–54.

members and on the rest of the social system? Contemporary sociologists, in their very proper concern with the accurate measurement of class indicators and their preoccupation with the interrelations among these indicators, have seriously neglected the important questions about the social consequences of different class structures which many earlier sociologists had placed at the center of their interest. The problem of the relations between classes, most strikingly illustrated in Marx' theory of the ubiquitousness of class struggle in all known societies, has been much neglected.

More recently these questions have begun to regain the attention they deserve. For example, S. M. Lipset in his *Political Man* used information on contemporary aspects of economic development to test an idea which we can trace to Aristotle, that "a society divided between a large impoverished mass and a small favored elite results either in oligarchy (dictatorial rule of the small upper stratum) or in tyranny (popular based dictatorship)." [26] Using indices of wealth such as per-capita income, levels of industrialization, urbanization, and education, Lipset shows conclusively that where there is greater wealth more widely shared, there the likelihood that democracy will develop and prevail is greatest. (The basic facts are summarized in Table 4.) Considering the relation of these facts to the class struggle, Lipset concludes:

> Economic development, producing increased income, greater economic security, and widespread higher education, largely determines the form of the 'class struggle,' by permitting those in the lower strata to develop longer time perspectives and more complex and gradualist views of politics. A belief in secular reformist gradualism can be the ideology of only a relatively well-to-do lower class. . . . Among the eight . . . wealthiest nations . . . all of whom had a per capita income of over $500 a year in 1949 . . . the Communists [did not] secure more than 7 per cent of the vote. . . . In the eight European countries which were below the $500 per capita income mark . . . the Communist Party . . . has had . . . an over-all average of more than 20 per cent . . . .[27]

[26] S. Martin Lipset, *Political Man* (New York: Doubleday, 1960), pp. 51–54.
[27] *Ibid.*, p. 61.

Class systems may influence other aspects of social structure, but they may also be shaped by them. Here we reverse the order of influence and ask, as our seventh question: What type of society is likely to produce what kind of stratification system? One of the most interesting propositions, put forth by Max Weber but not systematically tested since, is that in times of economic stability the stratification system would most likely rest mainly on considerations of prestige, but in times of rapid economic change stratification will more likely be based mainly on economic class factors. As Weber put it: "Every technological repercussion and economic transformation threatens stratification by status and pushes the class situation into the foreground." [28]

The sociologists' attempt to answer these seven questions, even if successful, does not settle the moral and political issues raised by social stratification. The justice or injustice of different systems of stratification and the possibility that men may someday form a society in which all are equal in possessions and in value will continue to agitate men, to excite their conscience, and to engage them politically. But the knowledge which sociologists have acquired and are now developing about systems of stratification in society can certainly help to establish the discussion of these issues on a firmer basis of fact.

Social Change

No aspect of social life is more challenging than the process of change, yet there are few other problems about which contemporary sociologists seem to have so little to say. Some critics attribute this to a conservative bias among leading contemporary sociologists. This allegedly leads them to stress the appropriateness of existing social arrangements, rather than to face up to the contradictions in contemporary society and to explore the prospects of changing it for the better. A more charitable interpretation would stress the shift of sociological interest from historical or long-range to contemporary and short-range problems, and from the comparative perspective to greater emphasis on the structure of the single society and even smaller units.

It has become popular, indeed fashionable, to say that sociologists lack a theory of social change. It would be more accurate to say that in the study of change, sociologists suffer not from too little but from too much theory. No other problem in social science has quite the same power to generate global theories which attempt to explain all else in social life by reference to one master key. The Marxian theory of history, which predicates all change in social life on the prior changes in the relations of people to the mode of production, is but one of a long list of examples. Sociology has largely turned its back on such global theories of change. Yet it is quite misleading to say that sociologists are not concerned with the problems of change, nor that they are without theory to account for it. Sociologists have abandoned the search for a single, all-encompassing theory of change. Instead, they seek to deal with change more concretely, one might say more realistically, as it manifests itself in different types of social organization under various conditions. Several examples, ranging from the smallest to the largest social units, may serve to illustrate the point.

In the study of attitudes and values, sociologists seek to discover the forces which produce changes in these important and generally stable personal

[28] Hans Gerth and C. Wright Mills (trans. and eds.), *From Max Weber: Essays in Sociology* (New York: Oxford University Press, 1946), p. 194.

orientations and dispositions. In a well-known study of college girls at Bennington College in Vermont, Theodore Newcomb sought to explain why some girls gave up their more conservative views under the influence of the college's "liberal" faculty, while others continued to adhere to the more conservative values of their original home and community. The girls who changed the most, Newcomb discovered, were those "characterized by independence from their parents, [a] sense of personal adequacy in social relations, and modifiability of habits of achieving their goals." [29]

Working in a very different environment, W. F. Cottrell asked what happens to people's values when the one industry on which they depend for their livelihood, and indeed on which they based the very existence of the entire community, is suddenly, totally, and apparently irretrievably lost to them. In his article "Death by Dieselization," Professor Cottrell describes the reactions of people living in a small community in the western desert, which had been developed entirely around the technological needs of the steam engine.[30] Such engines required servicing stations at intervals of 200 miles. When the transcontinental railroads switched to the diesel, which did not require attention at intermediate points across the desert, the entire economic basis of existence of these engine-servicing towns was eliminated in one sweep. Although the townsmen had earlier been deeply loyal to the railroad, many now became very critical of the presumed heartlessness of big business. Whereas they formerly made a great deal of the traditional American value of autonomy, independence, and standing on one's own feet, they now began to hope for and request numerous forms of government aid. Formerly they had sanctified the ideals of the private-property philosophy, but one now heard numerous ideas expressed which, if not quite socialistic in tone, at least seriously questioned the justice of allowing the pursuit of profit and "blind" market mechanisms to determine the course of economic events.

The study of change in institutions is well-represented by the work of sociological students of the family, who have been concertedly seeking an answer to the question: What changes occur in the family under the impact or urbanization and economic modernizations? The attack on this problem has been carried forward on a truly international basis, and a number of tentative answers seem likely to endure the scrutiny of further testing. These investigations reveal that throughout the world the process of modernization has tended to strengthen the nuclear family as against the extended family; to increase the degree of mutual sharing of responsibility between the spouses, in contrast to the more traditional sharp differentiation of responsibility by sex; and to encourage the free choice of partner by the individual, rather than by his parents or some other authority. At the same time, these studies reveal that even under modern conditions there is much strength left in the extended family, as reflected in patterns of residence and of mutual help; that some forms of dominance, notably by the men, persist to a surprising degree even in the most modern households; and that the choice of marital partner is usually restricted to narrowly defined traditional groups of "eligibles." [31]

[29] Theodore Newcomb, *Personality and Social Change* (New York: Dryden, 1948), p. 176.

[30] W. F. Cottrell, "Death by Dieselization," *American Sociological Review* (1951), XVI:358–365.

[31] See, for example, the special issue on "Changes in the Family," in *International Social Science Journal* (Paris: UNESCO, 1962), XIV:411–580.

Contemporary sociologists have not neglected the study of change in large-scale societies. Numerous attempts are currently in progress to trace the changes which the worldwide process of industrialization is introducing into traditional societies. Professors Wilbert Moore and Arnold Feldman report that there is a common core of structural elements found in industrial societies ranging from the more obvious features, such as a factory system of production and increasing urbanization, through "common cognitive orientations, such as the view of time and the uses of knowledge; [and] common value orientation, such as achievement orientation." [32] At the same time, they caution that there is no evidence that as societies become more industrial they become more alike in all respects, and point particularly to the fact that industrialization occurs under, and seems compatible with, both democratic and totalitarian political systems.

Despite the diversity in the units we have examined and the different kinds of change they reflect, these illustrations point to a set of elements and problems common to the study of social change. Probably the greatest ambiguity results from failure to specify the unit of change—that is, whether we speak of mankind and all world culture, of a particular society, one institution, a set of relationships, or some individual. Second, we must specify the elements we believe to be changing. For example, if we study change in a person, do we refer to his attitudes and values, his behavior, as in voting, or his social standing, as judged by his occupation? Third, it is necessary to agree about precisely what will be objectively accepted as constituting "change." A great many discussions about social change bog down in unresolved argument about whether certain changes, say in the rate of social mobility, are "real changes" or merely "expressions in new form" of older, well-documented characteristics.

A fourth set of problems arises from our efforts to measure the rate and direction of change. Some rates are obvious but relatively unambiguous —for example, the rate of growth in per-capita income. To measure the rate at which a population is becoming "modern in spirit," however, is infinitely more difficult. Measuring the "direction" of change is no less troublesome a task. The classical form which this question takes is: Is mankind progressing or regressing? Perhaps less interesting, but more amenable to study, are questions about the direction of change cast in less global and ambiguous terms—for example: Are the members of society becoming more or less interdependent? Are the populations of the several nations of the modern world developing a more-or-less common, world-wide, industrial culture?

Important as these issues are, they are, perhaps, all subordinate to the key question: What are the *causes* of social change? Sociologists are often able to establish that two elements of social life vary simultaneously, but they are much less often able to establish clear-cut sequences of events. They are even less successful in proving that they have isolated the *causal* factor in such sequences. The definitive establishment of causes is rendered difficult by the multiplicity of factors which operate in most social situations. Furthermore, sociologists are ordinarily not able to follow the example of the natural sciences, by developing controlled experiments to isolate the effect of single causes.[33]

[32] Wilbert Moore and Arnold Feldman, "Industrialization and Industrialism: Convergence and Differentiation," *Transactions of the Fifth World Congress of Sociology* (Louvain: International Sociological Association, 1962), II:165.

[33] We return to this issue in the next chapter, where we discuss the controversy about whether sociology is a science.

Sociologists may properly feel gratified that by improving the design of their research, developing more exact and reliable forms of measurement, and persistently clarifying their concepts, they are making some progress in increasing our understanding of the process of social change. Instead of the single, all-encompassing theory of change so notable a feature of classical sociology, we now have numerous theories of change which take account of the specific characteristics of different social units. We may have lost some sweep, and, perhaps, grandeur, but we are well-compensated by increases in the reliability and validity of the judgments we make.

seven

modes of inquiry in sociology

After settling for ourselves what sociology is about, developing a satisfactory conception of man and society, and choosing a problem to study, we still must make important decisions about how to go about investigating the problem we have selected. Once again, persons new to the field will find that the alternatives are numerous and that there is no unanimity among sociologists in accepting some one mode of analyzing social issues above all others. Instead, there is a continuing, and sometimes intense, debate. This debate is not limited to the evaluation of techniques, but rather deals with fundamental issues. Sociologists divide on the issue of whether sociology is or even can be a science, whether its method should be that of sympathetic understanding or the controlled experiment, whether it is nobler to build theory or to get one's hands dirty digging into the facts, whether sociology should be politically engaged or value-free. The decisions which sociologists make with regard to these issues have a profound effect on the kind of sociological investigations they conduct. To grasp fully what many sociologists are trying to do, and equally to understand the criticism which is sometimes directed against their work, one must know why these issues are important and what are some possible resolutions of the challenges they pose to sociological inquiry.

Is a Science of Society Possible?

Perhaps the most fundamental question which divides sociologists, one which largely subsumes all the others, concerns the status of sociology as science. There are really two questions here: Should sociology *try* to be a science? If so, is it able to meet the standards of science as we understand them today?

Sociology had its roots in social philosophy, which was most definitely not a science by contemporary standards. But in the era which included the formative years of sociology, the idea of science was all powerful; it bestowed the highest prestige on everything. Comte always spoke of sociology as science; indeed he assigned it first place as the "queen of sciences." The ideal of science, thus established, has held sway ever since. As long ago as 1873, Spencer was arguing the question "Is There a Social Science?" [1] against attacks very similar to those we can read today in the magazine section of Sunday's *New York Times.*[2]

There has always been a minority of sociologists, however, who regard sociology as essentially a humanistic branch of study, concerned with evaluation, criticism, and sympathetic understanding rather than with the usual pursuits of science. Often they seem to regard sociology as more a branch of history or politics than as a separate discipline. They are likely to point to the fact that Weber classified sociology not with the natural sciences, but with history and the social studies. Numerous contemporary sociologists hold to some variant of this position. C. W. Mills, for example, urged that sociology strive to be a "craft" rather than a science. Control and prediction, he said, are the concerns of a new bureaucratic type of sociologist who is departing from the old ideal.[3] Robert Bierstedt said in his 1960 Presidential Address to the Eastern Sociological Society: "Sociology owns a proper place not only among the sciences, but also among the arts that liberate the human mind." [4]

Those who wish sociology to be a humanistic discipline rather than a science base their argument on more than mere preference. They maintain that there are inherent limitations on the study of social phenomena which preclude sociology's attainment of true scientific status. They argue that the most important events are unique, that social phenomena do not follow "natural laws," and that the application of scientific methods to social events usually destroys the essential meaning of the events.

The Unique vs. the Recurrent

There cannot be a "science" of a single event. Science deals with the laws which govern recurrent or multiple events. Yet the most important events to which sociology should address itself, in the view of the humanist-sociologist, are precisely the unique historical forces and acts which have most shaped the course of human experience. Pitirim Sorokin forcefully expressed this idea when he said:

[1] Herbert Spencer, *The Study of Sociology* (New York: D. Appleton, 1929), pp. 22–42.

[2] Russell Kirk, "Is Social Science Scientific?", *New York Times* (June 25, 1961), Sec. 6:11 *ff*; Robert K. Merton, "Now the Case *for* Sociology," *New York Times* (July 16, 1961), Sec. 6:14; Russell Kirk, "The Battle of Sociology," *New York Times* (July 23, 1961), Sec. 6:30; Letters, *New York Times* (August 6, 1961), Sec. 6:52.

[3] C. Wright Mills, *The Sociological Imagination* (New York: Oxford University Press, 1959), pp. 113–117.

[4] Robert Bierstedt, "Sociology and Humane Learning," *American Sociological Review* (1960), XXV:3.

> I, for one, cannot see how we can operationally define and study such phenomena as the state; the nation; Taoism or Christianity; Classicism or Romanticism in the fine arts; epic, comedy, or tragedy; love or hatred; happiness or despair, or, as a matter of fact, any of the events of the whole past history of mankind. These historical events in all their uniqueness (for example, the murder of Julius Caesar) have already happened and cannot be reproduced in any present or future "operational" setting.[5]

Although there is some merit to this argument, it does not settle the issue. Science does not always treat repeated or recurrent events. The Ice Age or the Jurassic Period in geology, the birth of the solar system in astronomy, were unique events of momentous significance; but they are not thereby beyond our powers of scientific study and explanation. Furthermore, reference to the "uniqueness" of historical acts often obscures the fact that events such as the murder of Caesar, however individually unique, are also concrete historical manifestations of a larger class which may be numerous enough to support scientific generalization. The world has known no small number of dictators, and, of these, a not inconsiderable proportion have met violent ends. There is every reason to argue, therefore, even with regard to the death of dictators, that there may be sufficient examples of important historical events to support scientific generalization.[6] As Morris Cohen said: "The fact that social material is less repeatable than that of natural science, creates greater difficulty in verifying social laws but it does not abrogate the common ideal of all science." [7]

Of course, the sociologist who makes an historical generalization may easily fall into the error of assuming that any particular instance follows the form and detail of the general case. This happens often enough to be very disturbing to those who are aware of the distinct, even unique, characteristics of important historical events, and leads them to the often well-justified complaint that contemporary sociologists lack a "sense of history." Nevertheless, those more interested in history often completely fail to understand the nature of the process of scientific generalization. The effort to discover recurrent aspects of the death of dictators, and to expose the relations between such aspects, can be an end in itself. Such effort produces that special form of knowledge which is typical of science. The statement of a statistical regularity is not an attack on the idea of uniqueness. In presenting statistical generalizations we are not asserting that any particular selected case must be like all others. And it is often forgotten that knowledge of the general can greatly facilitate our understanding of the particular.

Even if we were to allow that the historically unique event is beyond science, it would not follow that there could be no scientific sociology. If sociology were to give up all claim to the analysis of the key events of history, such as the murder of Caesar, it would still have as subject matter all the myriad forms of social relationship which do recur and indeed have been repeated daily through the ages. In the relations of nation to nation and people to people in commerce and war, in procreation and kinship, in authority and subordination, in teaching and learning, and in all other aspects of social life, there is no end of recurrent social events which provide the subject matter for a scientific sociology. Our difficulty lies, indeed, not in

[5] Pitirim A. Sorokin, *Fads and Foibles in Modern Sociology and Related Sciences* (Chicago: Regnery, 1956), p. 50.

[6] George W. F. Hallgarten, *Why Dictators?* (New York: Macmillan, 1954).

[7] Morris Cohen, *Reason and Nature: An Essay on the Meaning of Scientific Method* (New York: Macmillan, 1931), p. 345.

having so few recurrent acts to analyze but so many. When we consider our resources and our past accomplishment, the magnitude of the task looms exceedingly large.

The Possibility of Social Laws

The prospect for a scientific sociology rests not only on the argument that social events are recurrent but also on the belief that they are regular or "lawful." This assumption was long ago set down by Durkheim as "the line" for all sociologists. Writing the preface to the first issue of *L'Année Sociologique* he said: "All doctrines . . . concern us, provided they admit the postulate which is the condition of any sociology, namely, that laws exist which reflection, carried out methodically, enables us to discover." [8]

After some 70 years of trying, sociologists are no longer so sanguine about the possibility that they can discover the laws of social phenomena. Indeed, Morris Cohen makes the stark suggestion that there may not be any social laws. Cohen acknowledges that social phenomena are determined, and in that sense are like all other natural phenomena. But in the case of physical laws, we have "relatively simple analytic functions containing a small number of variables," whereas in social phenomena we must deal with so large a number of variables organized in such complex patterns of interrelationship, as to seem "to a finite mind in limited time [not to] display any laws at all." [9]

The sociology books do, of course, contain references to numerous laws. Durkheim's law, that the suicide rate varies inversely with the degree of social integration characteristic of any group, is perhaps the best known. It is certainly one of the more precise and best established. Even this law suffers from a defect which is more painfully evident in the numerous social laws with which the history of sociology is studded. Laws are inherently abstract. They state what would be true if all other things remain equal. Although this often happens in the physical world, it almost never does in the social. One sociologist may prove, in one field of human action or with one population, that people respond to their economic interests; yet another can establish that they are influenced by their religion; whereas a third may show that education shapes the response in question; and a fourth will soon demonstrate that age plays a role, and so on at great length. Our failure to develop simple sociological laws may, therefore, be largely a reflection of the staggering complexity of social phenomena.

As sociology has developed in the recent past, it has shown a marked tendency to produce ever more complicated versions of what were initially simple theories describing how "x varies with y." Professor Robin Williams, in his presidential address to the American Sociological Association in 1958, pointed out that we no longer accept the classic and simple hypotheses we once favored. He pointed out, for example, that we were once satisfied to explain mutual personal attraction by the statement: "the greater the frequency of interaction between any two persons, the more likely it is that there will be mutual attraction, all other things being the same." [10] Our more sophisticated contemporary researcher will now propose that: "Within an interaction situation, friendship formation will be more likely to occur the

[8] Kurt H. Wolff (ed.), *Émile Durkheim, 1858–1917: A Collection of Essays, with Translations and a Bibliography* (Columbus: Ohio State University Press, 1960), p. 345.
[9] Cohen, *Reason and Nature*, p. 356.
[10] Robin Williams, "Continuity and Change in Sociological Study," *American Sociological Review* (1958), XXIII:624.

longer the situation occurs, the more often it is repeated, the more intimate it is, the less [the] competition that is involved, the more relaxed the atmosphere, and the more need there is for mutual activity." [11]

What was once beautifully simple has now become devilishly complex. If it is this staggering complexity of social phenomena which stands in the way of sociological progress, the answer *may lie* in modern mathematical modes of analysis and in the electronic computing machines which, unlike the "finite mind" of man, are undaunted by unlimited complexity. Of course, the machines can perform their unique function of rapidly processing large amounts of extremely complex data only if we can succeed in measuring social interaction in sufficient detail and with great precision. Unfortunately, with a few exceptions, we are still far from being able to thus "operationalize" our observation and recording of social phenomena. Nevertheless, some will take encouragement from Professor Herbert Simon's belief in the promise which mathematics holds for mastering the complexity of social phenomena: "Mathematics has become the dominant language of the natural sciences not because it is quantitative—a common delusion—but primarily because it permits clear and rigorous reasoning about phenomena too complex to be handled in words. This advantage of mathematics over cruder languages should prove of even greater significance in the social sciences, which deal with phenomena of the greatest complexity, than it has in the natural sciences." [12]

The Conflict of Meaning and Measurement

To the degree that social science requires ever greater precision, objective measurement, mathematical expression, and machine processing, it encounters with increasing vigor the charge that it distorts or even becomes emptied of meaning. Weber held it to be the distinction of social science that "we can accomplish something which is never attainable in the natural sciences, namely the subjective understanding of the action of the component individuals. The natural sciences . . . cannot do this. . . . We do not 'understand' the behavior of cells, but can only observe the relevant functional relationships and generalize on the basis of these observations." [13] Sorokin expressed similar concern about the loss of meaning which he feels results when the sociologist does not directly experience the social situations he analyzes, which is very often the case with those whose penchant is for the statistical manipulation of data. "Only through direct empathy," Sorokin argues, ". . . can one grasp the essential nature and difference between a criminal gang and a fighting battalion; between a harmonious and a broken family." [14]

No doubt statistical manipulation of depersonalized scores based on the ratings of observers who are not involved participants in some group can produce distortion or loss of meaning. The risks are no less great, however, in the work of the involved participant, whose very involvement in a situation weakens his ability to be an unbiased observer and analyst. We may put Professor Sorokin's assertion to a simple test, and one even more stringent than that he proposed. The difference between a criminal gang and a fighting

[11] Quoted in *American Sociological Review,* XXIII:624.

[12] Herbert A. Simon, *Models of Man: Social and Rational* (New York: Wiley, 1957), p. 89.

[13] Max Weber (A. Henderson and Talcott Parsons, trans.), *Theory of Social and Economic Organizations* (New York: Oxford University Press, 1947), p. 103.

[14] Sorokin, *Fads and Foibles,* p. 160.

battalion is after all rather obvious. It would, however, require a very sensitive instrument indeed to discriminate between two objectively similar discussion groups, each including 5 Harvard undergraduates, each assembled at random by the same recruiting method, and all discussing the same case study in human relations. Yet by using recently developed techniques, a qualified sociologist can now tell rather precisely, merely by glancing at a few statistics, which of two groups was "happy" and well-integrated, which tense and disintegrating. This can be done by using the records of group interaction scored by the method of Interaction Process Analysis.[15]

In Professor Bales' laboratory groups, 5 or 8 persons discuss a case in human relations—for example, whether a school principal should fire an extremely gifted teacher who has been flagrantly insubordinate. Since the discussion room in Bales' laboratory is faced by a two-way mirror, every action by each group member can be scored by trained observers as falling in 1 of 12 simple categories. When these scores are summed for all members of the group at the end of the hour-long discussion, the group's score on each of the 12 categories describes the group's "profile." [16]

Only a little experience with this method enables one to read fairly accurately from a group's profile what the spirit, temper, or morale of a given group was. Table 5 presents the action profiles of 2 discussion groups, each of 5 men. To simplify the presentation in this table, we have combined the data to yield 4 major categories. The 2 group profiles were chosen to present different degrees of group morale or cohesiveness. Morale in this case was measured by the extent to which the members of the group were satisfied with their participation, expressed positive feelings toward other group mem-

[15] Also see Chap. 3.

[16] Robert F. Bales, *Interaction Process Analysis* (Cambridge: Addison-Wesley, 1950), pp. 1–29.

Table 5

Action Profiles of Two Discussion Groups *

Action Category	*Percentage Group Morale*	
	High A	*Low* B
Questioning		
Asks for orientation, opinion, suggestion	4	10
Answering		
Gives orientation, opinion, suggestion	57	56
Positive		
Releases tension, shows solidarity or agreement	34	17
Negative		
Expresses tension, antagonism, disagreement	5	17
Total	100	100

* Adapted from Robert F. Bales, "The Equilibrium Problem in Small Groups," in Talcott Parsons, Robert F. Bales, and Edward Shils, *Working Papers in the Theory of Action* (Glencoe, Ill.: The Free Press, 1953), p. 116.

bers, and wanted to work further with members of the same group. Group A is a highly satisfied group, and B is a highly dissatisfied group.

We have no difficulty in identifying the groups simply by referring to their action profiles. *Positive* actions of an integrative variety, such as expressing agreement, are twice as common in the high-morale group (A) as in the low-morale group (B). *Negative* actions, such as expressing antagonism or disagreement, are three times as frequent in the low-morale as in the high-morale group. In the high-morale group, positive expressions are related to negative in the ratio 7:1, whereas in the low-morale group the ratio falls to 1:1. Notice also how much extra time Group B puts into asking questions, which reflects its inability to come to a quick understanding about facts and issues, and then to move on to the job of working out a solution to the human-relations problem the group has undertaken to solve.

Of course, an assessment of the morale in these groups could also have been made by a skilled participant observer trained to be sensitive to the nuances of group feeling. People with such skill are rare, however, whereas less talented people can learn to use the Bales technique for scoring interaction and rating the morale of groups. The Bales technique, furthermore, yields an objective factual record, so that the differences in interpretation which follow from differences in what observers believe is happening in a group are largely eliminated. The Bales technique also provides a permanent record; it is not necessary to have been there to evaluate a group's discussion. Finally, the Bales technique enables us to compare one group with another in an exact and precise way, which is often not possible when we simply talk about groups, especially when several observers have each worked with a different group and do not have a comon experience. It seems reasonable to say that the Bales technique of Interaction Process Analysis answers Professor Sorokin's challenge.

Conflict of Theory-Building and Empiricism

In many fields the interplay between theory and fact is rapid and intimate. Empirical work focuses on problems which theory shows to be important. Theory incorporates new empirical findings, gives them meaning by integrating them with other findings and existing theory, and on this basis points the way to new empirical research. Sociology has seldom enjoyed this happy condition. What it calls "theory" and "empirical research" are largely separate specialties. Sociology is not in this respect unique. In physics, for example, the theoretician generally does not do experimental work, and the experimentalists often describe themselves as being a breed quite different from the theoretical physicist. What is distinctive in sociology is that its theory is to a remarkable degree developed independently of any body of continuing research, and to an equal extent empirical research in sociology often has only limited connections with the concerns of the theorists.

The division is one of long standing. Weber called the two types "interpretive specialists" and "subject matter specialists." In a more derogatory spirit, C. W. Mills dubbed them the schools of "grand theory" and "abstracted empiricism," selecting Talcott Parsons as his prime example of the former and Paul Lazarsfeld as the epitome of the latter. These distinctions in the style of sociological work are so pervasive, and the feelings about them so strong, that one cannot effectively orient oneself in sociology without some awareness of the issues raised.

In part the division must be understood historically. Since sociology was an outgrowth of social philosophy, it tended to have a speculative and evaluative rather than an empirical investigative emphasis. Comte had an idea or scheme which he felt accounted for society and its development. The idea was its own justification. Although he understood the importance of testing his conceptions against the known facts, he really did not make a substantial effort to do so. At about the same time, in the mid-nineteenth century, there developed independently of the work of men like Comte and Spencer, and even to a degree in opposition to it, a concern with discovering the basic facts of social life. Thus, the first issue of the *Journal of the Statistical Society of London* in 1838 noted "a growing distrust of mere hypothetical theory and *a priori* assumption, and the appearance of a general conviction that, in the business of social science, principles are valid for application only inasmuch as they are legitimate induction from facts, accurately observed and methodically classified." [17]

The indifference of the great schematizers to facts, and the hostility of the early fact-gatherers to what they derisively called "mere figures of speech," provided competing models of sociological style for later generations. These contrasting approaches to sociological work continue, to an unfortunate degree, to compete for the allegiance of young sociologists. Undoubtedly, personal preference plays a major part in determining which role a young sociologist will take. Indeed, if the parts in this drama did not already exist, they would probably be invented again. But the fact that the script is already a standard feature of our experience makes it easy to take sides. Consequently, before he is very far along in his career, each young sociologist has pretty well committed himself to one of the competing positions.

In many ways the opposition of theory and empiricism is artificial and unreal, at least so far as it is applied to the contemporary scene. The battles are largely ideological, and often the most powerful thrusts are directed at straw men. There is the sound of much ripping, but in the nature of the case no real blood is drawn. The issues are greatly clarified if we avoid the slogans of people in different camps and make more precise distinctions about the types of work they actually do.

Robert Merton points out that under the heading of "theory" sociologists often lump one or more different types of work.[18]

1. Providing general orientation: Often the theorist is mainly concerned with identifying and making a case for the importance of a certain dimension or variable. He says in effect: "You ignore this order of fact at your peril." One example would be a social psychologist who argues that an investigation studying suicide should measure not only the degree of social integration of a group, but should also study the personality characteristics of its members. Another example would be the researcher studying small groups who urges that one pay attention not only to the effect which is produced by the rules governing group interaction but also that we consider the effect which the mere size of a group has on social processes within it. In the field of demography, it might be the man who stresses the importance of religion, or some similar value orientation, as an influence on the birth rate. In the study

[17] Nathan Glazer, "The Rise of Social Research in Europe," in D. Lerner (ed.), *The Human Meaning of the Social Sciences* (New York: Meridian, 1959), p. 50.

[18] Robert K. Merton, "The Bearing of Sociological Theory on Empirical Research," *Social Theory and Social Structure* (Glencoe, Ill.: The Free Press, 1957), p. 86. In the following pages I have not followed Professor Merton's scheme exactly, but rather have freely adapted it.

of social mobility, it could be the researcher who urges us not to forget the contribution IQ makes to getting ahead in the world. Ordinarily, no sociologist has any particular quarrel with this type of theory-building so long as the competition produced as people clamor for attention to *their* favorite variable does not interfere with his ability to win a hearing for the variables in which he personally is most interested.

2. Developing sociological concepts: Concepts are indispensable tools of any scientific inquiry, although in themselves they do not suffice as a basis for conducting research. Concepts specify the form and content of the variables which one's general sociological orientation defines as important. Thus, Durkheim not only assigned importance to the degree of social integration of a group, but he went on to define several types of integration, the best known described by the concept *anomie,* or a state of normlessness. Talcott Parsons does not limit himself to the idea that all behavior tends to be patterned. He also presents a set of concepts such as his pattern variables [19] which he finds necessary in order to do justice to the different aspects of the way in which people relate to one another.

Although such concepts are indispensable to any science, it is unfortunate that so many sociological theorists stop at this point. The more empirical-minded sociologist typically makes two complaints against this practice. First, he points out that while the theorist may have defined the concept, he frequently gives no precise indication of how one should go about trying to find out whether the thing defined actually exists in the real world. A second, and even more forceful, complaint is that the theorist frequently fails to indicate what one can do with his concepts other than use them as labels to replace the labels these same things already bear. As George Homans put it: "Much modern sociological theory seems to me to possess every virtue except that of explaining anything. Part of the trouble is that much of it consists of a system of categories, or pigeon-holes, into which the theorist fits different aspects of behavior." [20]

3. Formulating empirical generalizations: Following John Dewey, Merton defines an empirical generalization as "an isolated proposition summarizing observed uniformities of relationships between two or more variables." [21] As an example he cites Halbwachs' finding that laborers spend more per adult for food than do white-collar employees with the same size income. As Merton notes, sociological writing abounds in such empirical findings.[22] There are numerous new ones reported in every issue of the sociological journals. They are the chief product of the typical empirical researcher.

At this point, those with a stronger affinity for theory again find fault with the empiricist. We have endless facts, but they frequently contradict one another. The results emerging from research vary greatly depending on the conditions under which the study was conducted, the sample used, and the like. More serious, the findings do not necessarily add up; they do not give us cumulative knowledge and increasing power to predict or control. Indeed, our research findings often fail to yield even the encouraging feeling that we now better understand the phenomenon just studied. The dissatisfaction which many of the more theoretically oriented sociologists feel in

[19] The pattern variables were listed and defined in Chap. 3.

[20] George C. Homans, *Social Behavior: Its Elementary Forms* (New York: Harcourt, Brace & World, 1961), p. 10.

[21] Merton, *Social Theory and Social Structure,* p. 25.

[22] *Ibid.,* p. 95.

the face of the mounting tide of unconnected empirical findings was tersely expressed by Robert Lynd when he said: "Research without an actively selective point of view becomes the ditty bag of an idiot, filled with bits of pebbles, straws, feathers and other random hoardings." [23]

4. Elaborating scientific theory: What is wanted, of course, is not discrete findings, but a scientific law, what Merton defines as "a statement of inference derivable from a theory." [24] As Merton and every other sociologist is well aware, this type of sociological law is extremely rare. Our old friend Durkheim again comes to the rescue. His statement that suicide varies with the degree of integration of a social group is such a law. On the basis of it, one can safely predict which groups will have a higher suicide rate among those varying in religion, marital condition, sex, and level of education.

To explain why this law operates, we must understand a sequence of steps which makes clear the underlying logic of a set of relationships. Merton outlines them as follows:

1. Social cohesion provides psychic support to group members subjected to acute stresses and anxieties.
2. Suicide rates are functions of *unrelieved* anxieties and stresses to which persons are subjected.
3. Catholics [and specified additional groups] have greater social cohesion than Protestants.
4. Therefore, lower suicide rates should be anticipated among Catholics than among Protestants.[25]

Our ideal is to be always to complete the cycle leading from the development of such interrelated propositions to the generation of research designed to test them, then on to the subsequent revision of the theory in the light of the research findings, and then finally to the design of new research. In reality, as Merton notes, there are "marked discontinuities of empirical research, on the one hand, and systematic theorizing unsustained by empirical test, on the other." [26] It was not always thus, nor need it be so. Most contemporary sociologists recognize that the writing of the past masters such as Durkheim and Weber was dominated by theoretical interests even when it was most empirical in practice. Both *Suicide* and *The Protestant Ethic* are appropriate examples. We have, therefore, had to regain lost ground in working toward a proper appreciation of the relation of theory to research. It remains for the future generations of sociologists to attain in practice what many in the present generation understand well only in principle.

Sociology, Values, and Politics

The student of society is easily tempted to conclude that his specialized knowledge qualifies him to be the doctor of society, also its spiritual adviser, perhaps its planner, and even its director. Auguste Comte had a vision of a new form of society which would be based on knowledge drawn from the newly created science of sociology. In effect a complete moral transformation of mankind, he sketched in great detail a plan for a new Religion of Humanity to be directly by a priesthood having special

[23] Robert Lynd, *Knowledge for What?* (Princeton: Princeton University Press, 1939), p. 183.

[24] Merton, *Social Theory and Social Structure,* p. 96.

[25] *Ibid.*, p. 97.

[26] *Ibid.*, p. 99.

scientific knowledge of man and nature. The chilling implications of such "scientific" schemes for reforming mankind soon produced in many a deep-seated resolve to keep sociology separate from politics.

Durkheim sought to make the distinction between sociology and social doctrine as explicit as possible when he said, in *The Rules of Sociological Method:* "Sociology . . . will be neither individualistic, Communistic, nor socialistic. . . . On principle it will ignore these theories, in which it could not recognize any scientific value, since they tend not to describe or interpret, but to reform, social organization." [27] Similar precautions have been urged on the field by most of its leading figures. Pareto warned against the danger that the personal sentiments of the sociologist might lead him to report not "what is" but "what *ought* to be" in order "to fit in with his religious, moral, patriotic, humanitarian sentiments." [28] Weber, in his turn, urged that sociology remain "value-free." [29]

Although the aspiration toward a value-free or politically neutral sociology has been the dominant orientation among contemporary sociologists, a number of leading men have seriously challenged this position. Robert Lynd, co-author of the famous *Middletown* studies, made an impassioned plea for a more engaged social science in his Stafford Little Lectures at Princeton in 1938, which he published under the title *Knowledge for What?* Lynd rejected the ideal of a disinterested science, asserting that the social sciences were and always had been mainly tools, "instruments for coping with areas of strain and uncertainty in culture." He therefore urged social scientists to respond to the public need for policy guidance by coming out from behind the "sheltering tradition of 'scientific' objectivity." [30] Similar sentiments were echoed by C. W. Mills in his *Sociological Imagination* (1959), in which he bemoaned the loss of what he called sociology's "reforming push." Mills also alleged that contemporary sociology had failed to come to the defense of freedom and reason, both of which he considered gravely threatened in the modern world.[31] In pressing for this kind of social science, Lynd and Mills are joined by the great Swedish economist, Gunnar Myrdal, who addressed himself to this issue in brilliant article on "Social Theory and Social Policy." Here he said: "We need viewpoints, and they presume valuations. A 'disinterested social science' is from this viewpoint, pure nonsense. It never existed, and it will never exist." [32]

Not one but several different issues are raised by the plea of Lynd, Mills, and others for a more engaged sociology. At some points they stand on firm ground, at others they rest on shaky foundations. Rather than treat the problem at a general level, therefore, we are well-advised to consider the different dimensions separately.

We cannot contradict those who argue for a more engaged sociology when they insist that social research, like all scientific research, has practical consequences, and that these should be recognized. Neither can we success-

[27] Émile Durkheim (G. Catlin, ed.; S. Solovay and J. Mueller, trans.), *The Rules of Sociological Method*, 8th ed. (Chicago: University of Chicago Press, 1938), p. 142.

[28] From Vilfredo Pareto (T. Livingston, ed.), *Mind, Self and Society* (New York: Harcourt, Brace & World, 1939), quoted in V. F. Calverton (ed.), *The Making of Society* (New York: Modern Library, 1937), p. 545.

[29] See Alvin Gouldner, "Anti-Minotaur: The Myth of a Value-Free Sociology," *Social Problems* (1963), IX:199–213.

[30] Lynd, *Knowledge for What?* p. 114 *ff.*, 120.

[31] Mills, *The Sociological Imagination*, pp. 165–176.

[32] Gunnar Myrdal, "The Relation Between Social Theory and Social Policy," *British Journal of Sociology* (1953), XXIII:242.

fully challenge their assertion that values guide research, either consciously or unconsciously. Moreover, since unstated values are harder to identify and control, we should agree that it is best that the researcher make his values explicit. This is, of course, more easily said than done, since the values guiding a piece of research are not always consciously known to the researcher. More important, we must recognize that curiosity, the simple desire to know, is also a value.

Those who criticize social research because it is primarily motivated by intense moral or political values, and those who criticize it for not defending or advancing any particular political or social value at all, are equally missing what is for other sociologists the central point. For many sociologists the prime consideration is the advancement of knowledge. There is no guarantee that useful knowledge and understanding will more surely emerge from politically engaged research than from that which purports to be neutral. The crucial question is not what led a man to a problem, but what he does about it. The loftiest motives may produce the most sterile research, and "idle" curiosity the most challenging findings. The critical issue is whether the actual conduct of the research and the presentation of evidence follow the rules set down by scientific procedure, conceiving science in the broadest rather than in narrower terms.

Myrdal is right when he says: "Chaos does not organize itself into any cosmos. We need viewpoints." [33] But can it be that the only permissible viewpoint is that of traditional liberal philosophy, the only important motivation compassion for human suffering or the pursuit of reason? Does not the scientist have a right to aloofness? We should not forget Professor Cohen's reminder that "the aloofness involved in the pursuit of pure science is the condition of that liberality which makes man civilized." [34]

The activist not only argues that we should let our values guide our research, but he also tells us what those values should be. First and foremost, we must be critical of the status quo. Thus, Robert Lynd says it is "the role of the social sciences to be troublesome, to disconcert the habitual arrangements by which we manage to live along, and to demonstrate the possibility of change in more adequate directions." [35]

Any social-science investigation, merely by laying bare the facts of social existence, may bring the sociological investigator under attack for undermining cherished belief or for questioning established truth. Although every sociologist must accept this risk, it seems going too far to insist that his *objective* must be to incur it. Why should not his purpose equally be to approve, to conserve, and to integrate? Either purpose, or neither, the choice seems a matter of personal or political preference. In a civilized world a man should be free to choose the position he finds congenial. As a politically active person you may criticize him for his inactivity. But as a sociologist your evaluation of him should rest on the quality and adequacy of his sociological research. The universal standard of judgment for that purpose is the degree to which he advances knowledge of man and society.

The activist will respond by saying that we make a serious mistake if we place in opposition "good" sociological research and politically motivated research because "good" research is that which finds solutions to the pressing practical problems facing the world. The choice of almost any other kind of problem is treated by those who incline to the activist view as either escape

[33] *Loc. cit.*
[34] Cohen, *Reason and Nature*, p. 350.
[35] Lynd, *Knowledge for What?*, p. 181.

or timidity. Even if this diagnosis were correct, those who prefer to work on other problems are still entitled to their choice. If the activists had their way, we might ultimately be led to "directed" research in which some public authority would choose the problems on which social scientists should, and indeed must, work. Anyone with even the faintest knowledge of totalitarian countries such as Soviet Russia or Nazi Germany knows that this means the initial perversion and ultimately the complete destruction of social science. Even in a democratic society, as Morris Cohen points out, "To subordinate the pursuit of truth to practical considerations is to leave us helpless against bigoted partisans and fanatical propagandists who are more eager to make their policies prevail than to inquire whether or not they are right." [36]

Even if we accept the demand that sociology's first obligation is to help solve social problems, it by no means follows that the surest way to such solutions is to devote our attention exclusively to such matters. To do so would be analogous to arguing that the spread of cancer is so serious that one should not waste time studying the biochemistry of growth in the normal cell. As Cohen again reminds us: "The social reformer, like the physician, the engineer, and the scientific agriculturalist, can improve the human lot only to the extent that he utilizes the labor of those who pursue science for its own sake regardless of its practical applications." [37]

In the end, then, the issue comes down to that of the legitimacy of pure science. Those who urge an engaged, critical, practical, problem-centered sociology certainly have every right to their preference. More than that, it may well be that in the social sciences, as against the natural, research focused on practical problems will in the end prove more productive. Where the activist goes wrong is in questioning the legitimacy of any other kind of social science, especially the kind which aspires to meet the conditions of pure science. The ideal of pure science, especially pure social science, may in fact be unattainable. "The only answer," again in the words of Morris Cohen, "is that this is true also of the ideal of beauty, of holiness, and of everything else that is ultimately worth while and humanly ennobling." [38]

Summary

Sociologists are often embarrassed and distressed by their pervasive disagreements, thinking that this reflects poorly on the maturity of their field. They fail to realize that debates concerning the way in which inquiry should be conducted are endemic in science. In a remarkable paper called "What Do Scientists Do?" Joseph J. Schwab reported the results of his review of some 4,000 scientific papers written by European and American scientists over a span of almost 5 centuries.[39] The research he examined was mainly in biology, psychology, and the behavioral sciences; and his purpose was to explore the debates among scientists about how their inquires *should* be conducted.

Professor Schwab's investigation led him to conclude that the issues raised and the positions adopted in debates about the modes of scientific enquiry were "remarkably constant from science to science and from epoch to epoch." [40] Moreover, he reached the rather surprising conclusion that the choices scientists made between alternative modes of inquiry were not the

[36] Cohen, *Reason and Nature*, p. 350.
[37] *Ibid.*, pp. 349–350.
[38] *Ibid.*, p. 350.
[39] Joseph J. Schwab, "What Do Scientists Do?" *Behavioral Science* (1960), V:1–27.
[40] *Ibid.*, p. 1.

product of the "inexorables of logic or of history" but rather must be accounted for by personal preferences based on personality factors and the "ephemerals of circumstance." It does no good to look to Professor Schwab for some reliable method of ascertaining, in the light of the history of science, which is *the* best or most productive approach, since he concluded that "there are many ways of achieving mastery of a subject of enquiry, no one of them capable of undebatable superiority over the others; each of them capable of illuminating the world of things in a way not precisely duplicated by the others." [41]

Professor Schwab's work suggests how wise we would be to resist the temptation to squander our energies in squabbles over which is the *true* or the *best* method of sociological inquiry. Recognizing that each method has a contribution to make, we should adopt a more catholic and tolerant attitude toward approaches different from those to which we personally incline. The critical question is not so much what is a man's ideology of research but rather what is the extent of his contribution to knowledge. Understandably, people become emotionally committed to their scientific positions. Often they can no more accept the inevitable tentativeness of their pet method or theory than they can face up to the fact of their own mortality. We do well, therefore, to remember Pareto's dispassionate analysis:

> The logico experimental sciences are made up of a sum of theories that are like living creatures, in that they are born, live, and die, the young replacing the old, the group alone enduring. As is the case with living beings, the lifetimes of theories vary in length and not always are the long-lived ones the ones that contribute most to the advancement of knowledge. Faith and metaphysics aspire to an ultimate resting place. Science knows that it can attain only provisory, transitory positions. Every theory fulfills its function, and nothing more can be asked of it.[42]

[41] *Ibid.*, p. 23.
[42] Calverton (ed.), *The Making of Society*, p. 539.

sociology as a profession

eight

Sociology is not only an intellectual discipline; it is also a profession. When we consider any branch of learning as an intellectual discipline, we have in mind the premises on which the men in the field rest their work, the ideas and currents of thought which unite or separate them, the characteristic styles of reasoning or argument which they use, the types of data considered, the way in which they are collected, and the manner in which they are treated. When we speak of a profession, we refer mainly to such themes as the uses or applications of a body of knowledge—for example, whether to teach or to heal; to the context in which the discipline is used, whether in public or privately, with large groups or face to face with one individual; to the way in which those concerned with a given realm make their living; how they are related to their "client," to one another, and to the larger society; how much freedom and autonomy they enjoy; how well or poorly organized they are, and the like. The nature and practice of a discipline determine the kind of intellectual enterprise and profession it may become.

Sociology as a Teaching Profession

Teaching absorbs by far the largest part of the nation's sociological energies. Approximately three fourths of those holding the Ph.D. in sociology teach in university or college programs. Professional schools, especially of education and social work, but increasingly those of business, law, and medicine as well, also employ sociologists as teachers. Of those sociologists with an academic connection, 1 in 8 is affiliated with a professional school, a research institute within a university, or an other-than-sociology teaching department.[1]

The development of sociology in American universities is distinguished by the following facts: it came very late to the academic scene; its bearers could neither point to a well-established and venerable intellectual tradition, nor claim for themselves superior and distinguished personal social origins; and it nevertheless grew at a phenomenal rate. These facts played an important role both in shaping the reception sociology received in the American academic community and the reaction of sociologists to that reception.

Growth of Sociology in America

All of the social studies had to struggle to win a place for themselves in the traditional or classical program of the American college and university. The task was probably easiest for history, which could trace its origins to Herodotus and readily pass for a humane branch of learning. Economics was less readily accepted, but the distinction of Adam Smith and the importance of the subject to English and American societies undergoing rapid economic development greatly smoothed the way. Sociology came along at the end of this chain of development. The first department of sociology was not established until 1893 at Chicago. The American Sociological Association was formed by a rump group which broke away from the parent Economic Association in 1905.[2] Although Spencer's evolutionary theory had had some vogue in the United States, very few people had at the time heard of sociology and fewer still knew the meaning of this strange new term only recently coined.

The newer Midwestern colleges and universities, state supported and generally more democratic, welcomed the new discipline and it grew up along with them. Yet sociology was by no means excluded in the East. Brown, Columbia, Dartmouth, Pennsylvania, and Yale introduced sociology courses prior to the founding of the Sociological Society, and Yale was host to William Graham Sumner, one of the first of the great American sociologists. There were, however, major pockets of resistance to this new and strange discipline among the more conservative, private and elite eastern schools. Harvard did not establish a department of sociology until Sorokin came to the University in 1930. It is striking that as late as 1960, 5 of the nation's 20 "leading" liberal arts colleges [3] still did not offer any instruction in sociology.

Sociology's late arrival on the academic scene was compensated for neither by the social standing of its partisans nor the inherent status of its subject matter. Very few representatives of the older and wealthier families of the eastern seaboard took up sociology as they did the classics, literature, or history. The early American sociologists were distinctively products of the rural rather than the urban segment of the country. Almost without exception the first two dozen presidents of the American Sociological Association were of rural origin. So pervasive was this characteristic that C. W. Mills detects in the work of American students of social pathology a typical rural prejudice against the city, a tendency to see it as the source and natural home of vice,

[1] Elbridge Sibley, *The Education of Sociologists in the United States* (New York: Russell Sage Foundation, 1963).

[2] Roscoe C. Hinkle, Jr., and Gisela J. Hinkle, *The Development of Modern Sociology* (New York: Random House, 1954), p. 3 *ff*.

[3] Liberal arts colleges are classified as leading if, among each 1,000 graduates, 15 or more won fellowships or earned the Ph.D.

crime, broken families and the like.[4] The rural origins of the early sociological leaders frequently combined with a connection with the ministry. A surprisingly high proportion of the early sociologists were descended from ministers or were themselves trained in the ministry. The list includes such outstanding figures as Lester Ward, early disciple of Comte and often regarded as the father of American sociology, Franklin Giddings, founder and long-time head of the Department of Sociology at Columbia, Albion Small, founder and chairman of the great department at Chicago, and many others.

The early sociologists in Europe dealt mainly with theories of history or drew on the lives of primitives to illustrate their ideas about evolution, religion, and society. Although similar themes and sources figured prominently in the work of Ward and Sumner, early American sociology gave a much greater share of its attention to the pressing social problems which seemed to spring up everywhere in the rapidly changing American society. This was especially true at the University of Chicago, which for more than two decades (1915–1940) was virtually unchallenged as the leading center of sociological training in America. Chicago sociologists in the living laboratory provided by the city studied the slum and ghetto, the prostitute and juvenile delinquent, the professional criminal, jazz, and drug addiction.[5]

Despite the plain origins of its practitioners and the often raw quality of its subject matter, or perhaps because of them, sociology grew rapidly, indeed phenomenally. The hundred-odd members who had founded the American Sociological Society in 1905 had increased almost sevenfold by the time the United States entered World War I. After the war it experienced another spurt of growth, more than doubling in size in the next 10 years. Although the number of members decreased during the depression years, the period after the Second World War saw the resumption of growth. Indeed, the membership of the Sociological Association has been growing in the postwar period at the exceptional rate of some 10 per cent a year, and in 1960 included more than 6,000.

There is hardly a college or university where sociology is not taught today. One study of a sample of 263 colleges revealed that they offered an average of about 14 courses in sociology at each school.[6] In 1958–1959 the U. S. Office of Education reported that 641 universities and colleges (exclusive of schools of social work) awarded bachelors degrees in sociology to almost 7,000 students graduating that year.[7] The number of graduates majoring in sociology is slightly larger than in political science and slightly smaller than in psychology and economics. In the face of such growing interest and increasing acceptance, sociologists have come to feel about their discipline much as Lavoisier did about chemistry when he said in 1805: "I do not expect my ideas to be adopted all at once. . . . Those who have

[4] C. Wright Mills, "The Professional Ideology of Social Pathologists," *American Journal of Sociology* (1943), XLIX:165–180.

[5] Some contributions from the Chicago School of Sociologists are: Robert Park, Edward W. Burgess, and R. D. McKenzie, *The City* (Chicago: University of Chicago Press, 1925); Nels Anderson, *The Hobo: The Sociology of the Homeless Man* (Chicago: University of Chicago Press, 1923); Louis Wirth, *The Ghetto* (Chicago: University of Chicago Press, 1929); Harvey Zorbaugh, *The Gold Coast and the Slum* (Chicago: University of Chicago Press, 1929); William I. Thomas, *The Unadjusted Girl* (Boston: Little, Brown, 1931); Clifford Shaw, *The Jack Roller* (Chicago: University of Chicago Press, 1930); Frederic Thrasher, *The Gang* (Chicago: University of Chicago Press, 1927).

[6] Lawrence Podell, Martin Vogelfanger, and Roberta Rogers, "Sociology in American Colleges," *American Sociological Review* (1959), XXIV:95.

[7] *Earned Degrees, Conferred, Bachelors' and Higher Degrees.* United States Office of Education (1958–1959), p. 179.

envisaged nature according to a certain point of view during much of their career, rise only with difficulty to new ideas. It is the passage of time, therefore, which must confirm or destroy the opinions I have presented. Meanwhile, I observe with great satisfaction that the young people . . . are beginning to study the science without prejudice. . . .[8]

The Undergraduate Curriculum

How far the academic image of sociology as a discipline is shaped by its course offerings is difficult to assess. Although it may not be important to those who spend full time on research, the curriculum certainly is one of the main concerns of the teaching sociologist.

The fare offered in most sociology departments is much less diversified than our initial survey of the field (Chap. 2) might indicate. A general introductory course in sociology (and also in anthropology in the common joint department) is ubiquitous. Beyond this the courses most commonly offered, in order of frequency, are: marriage and the family, criminology, social problems, social work, social "deviance," social psychology, and social theory. Together these 10 leading subjects account for approximately two thirds of all the courses regularly offered to undergraduates in sociology.[9] Since half of these can be considered part of one complex focused on the theme of personal and social adjustment, the degree of concentration is very great indeed. There is hardly a sociology department, however small, which does not offer one or more courses on this theme.

By contrast, many of the most important elements of social life, the chief social institutions and problems to which the founders of sociology gave a central place and which still loom so large in European sociology today, are gravely neglected in the sociology curriculum available to many American undergraduates. A course on social stratification, the sociology of religion, or economic sociology is available in only 1 of 10 departments, and a course on the sociology of politics in only 1 of 20.[10]

The teaching of sociology in American colleges therefore suffers from a peculiar condition. Those subjects which are most important in the intellectual tradition of the field, most emphasized in graduate instruction, and most often of interest to the instructors are seldom taught to undergraduates. To illustrate: The complex of courses which includes social work, public welfare, child welfare, and community organization ranks number 1 among undergraduate courses listings, but in frequency of choice as a field of special interest among sociologists it ranks fourteenth.[11] At the other end of the scale, we find that the field most often chosen as a specialty by sociologists, namely social psychology, ranks only seventh in course listings, and the second most-chosen specialization, "social organization," is in tenth place in the number of course offerings. As the authors of one of the surveys of this problem despairingly phrased their conclusion: "the further removed is the subject matter from the discipline of sociology, as it is defined in the first chapter in most introductory texts . . . the more courses [on it] are offered by departments of sociology."[12] Another put the matter more directly and

[8] Quoted in Charles C. Gillispie, *The Edge of Objectivity* (Princeton: Princeton University Press, 1960), p. 232.

[9] Podell, Vogelfanger, and Rogers, *American Sociological Review* (1959), XXIV:92.

[10] *Ibid.*, p. 9.

[11] Matilda White Riley, "Membership of the American Sociological Association," *American Sociological Review* (1960), XXV:925.

[12] Podell, Vogelfanger, and Rogers, *American Sociological Review* (1959), XXIV:95.

succinctly when he said: "the college courses given in sociology do not reflect the interests of those who teach them." [13]

Whatever the explanation, we cannot but be struck by the narrow range of sociological theory and research to which so many students are limited. No less peculiar is the situation of their instructors, who teach but a small part of what their discipline has to offer, and who in their teaching can neither carry forward the tradition of their discipline nor exercise the special skills which they acquired in their own graduate training.

Although these are striking facts, they hardly tell the whole story about sociology as a teaching profession. However narrow the limits of the courses they may offer, sociologists, almost without exception, find teaching their subject to be a richly rewarding experience. They give the student his first contact with a subject to which he has not previously been introduced in high school. Through this encounter he gains his first systematic appreciation, sometimes even his first awareness, of the structure of his society, of the nature of man's condition, and of the variety of solutions of human problems which societies have tried or may yet attempt. To be able to bring this experience to his students is sufficient to make most sociologists quite ready "to gladly teach."

Sociology as a Research Enterprise

With few exceptions sociologists make their living by teaching or research, or some combination of the two. Even those in administration usually work in the context of a university, a government agency, or a business corporation. The 1959 census of members of the American Sociological Association showed 70 per cent affiliated with universities and colleges, 5 per cent working for the federal government, 6 per cent employed by business and industry, and the remainder mainly in state and local organizations such as schools, hospitals, prisons, and the like.[14] Among those professions which it is reasonable to compare with sociology, this pattern is probably most like that for economists. Historians, by contrast, are found almost exclusively in teaching posts, whereas psychologists are found in large numbers in private practice, which is rare among sociologists.[15]

Unfortunately, we cannot trace this pattern very far back to discover its stability or variability. A census comparable to that for 1959 is available only for 1950.[16] Even over this short span, however, several trends emerge which are probably of long-term significance.

Between 1950 and 1959 the proportion of sociologists with a university or college affiliation decreased from 75 to 70 per cent of the total, while those with a government or other types of affiliation increased from 22 to 26 per cent.[17] While a shift of this magnitude hardly suggests a radical transformation of the profession, it points to the increasing representation of those engaged either in full-time research or in applications of sociology. This trend is strengthened by the fact that of those in colleges and universities, an increasing proportion is affiliated with professional schools. Such schools increased their share of sociological employment from 8 to 11 per cent.[18]

[13] Richard L. Simpson, "Expanding and Declining Fields in American Sociology," *American Sociological Review* (1961), XXVI:464.

[14] Riley, *American Sociological Review*, XXV:921.

[15] Molly Harrower, "Psychologists in Independent Practice," in B. Webb (ed.), *The Profession of Psychology* (New York: Holt, Rinehart and Winston, 1962), p. 130.

[16] Riley, *American Sociological Review*, XXV:921.

[17] *Loc. cit.*

[18] *Loc. cit.*

The available facts may be used to argue that sociology is becoming less exclusively an academic discipline or a pure science, and is more and more developing a major component of applied work.

Investment in Social Research

It is difficult to get figures on the extent of the nation's investment in sociological research, and more difficult still to assess those one does get. The available data describe expenditures for social science taken as a whole, and it is not feasible to judge what part of the total is accounted for by sociology alone. Even these figures are unfortunately limited to expenditures more or less explicitly earmarked for research in some institution's budget. We know, of course, that a great deal of social research is done under conditions likely to escape notice in anyone's research budget. Many a professor whose entire salary is charged to teaching spends three or more hours each day doing research in the library, the laboratory, or in the field. An adequate accounting system would certainly assign a value to this time and weigh it in the total. Despite such defects, the data available on expenditures for social-science research tell an interesting story.

Social-science research has become a large-scale affair. Dr. Harry Alpert, formerly Social Science Director at the National Science Foundation, estimates that in 1959 the total American expenditure for such research, both basic and applied, was $215 million.[19] This is less than half the cost of one atom-powered aircraft carrier and only a very small fraction of the total spent for research in the natural, physical, and engineering sciences. Indeed, the social sciences' share of the research budget of the federal government decreased from 24 per cent in 1937 to a mere 2 per cent in 1953. This did not mean an absolute decline in funds for social science, but rather came about because of the phenomenal increase in federal support of research in the physical and natural sciences. Indeed, the sum of $215 million represents a large increase in the absolute investment in social-science research. In this field the federal government spent only $17 million in 1937, but by 1953 the figure had risen to $53 million.[20]

It is not the federal government but industrial and commercial organizations which are the largest single source of funds for social-science research. In 1959 they accounted for $137 million, or almost 64 per cent of the total.[21] Some of this money was spent on studies of public opinion. The greatest part of it, however, went for "marketing research," a term used for investigations of the effects of advertising and of the preferences of consumers for one or another product or brand. The results of these studies are usually accessible only to the companies which pay for them. In any event, they would have little interest for most sociologists. We must, therefore, recognize that the largest outlay of moneys for social research contributes little or nothing to the general advance of social science. It may, of course, be argued that it is actually inappropriate even to include this type of expenditure with those used to support scientific research.

The federal government stands second as a source of social-science

[19] Harry Alpert, "The Growth of Social Research in the United States," in D. Lerner (ed.), *The Human Meaning of the Social Sciences* (New York: Meridian, 1959), p. 74.

[20] Milton Graham, *Federal Utilization of Social Science Research: Exploration of the Problem* (Washington, D.C.: The Brookings Institution, 1954), mimeographed report, p. 46.

[21] Alpert in D. Lerner (ed.), *The Human Meaning of the Social Sciences*, p. 75.

research funds. It provides one quarter of the money, spending the greater part directly and allocating the remainder to other organizations. A special study of social-science expenditure by the federal government was undertaken in 1953 by Dr. Milton Graham of the Brookings Institution, and it revealed some striking and distressing trends.[22]

Dr. Graham reported that the "research contract" had become the chief means by which the government allocated funds to support the work of non-profit research organizations such as universities. The contract, as against an unrestricted grant, usually calls for the performance of specifically defined research and the delivery of some particular report or other result. Most scientists feel that the contract system "indirectly but inevitably reduces the [number of] exploratory investigations, particularly in directions which are not in the spotlight at the moment." [23]

In 1952 only 6 per cent of the federal government funds for social science went to support basic research, whereas 44 per cent was spent on collecting general-purpose statistics such as census data, and 50 per cent was used for applied research.[24] Thus, in the social sciences as in the physical, we can see the operation of what Vannevar Bush, wartime Director of the Office of Scientific Research and Development, called "the perverse law" whereby "applied research invariably drives out pure." [25] Dr. Graham also pointed out that while virtually every department of the federal government now conducts some social-science research, and almost every branch of American life and every social problem receives some attention, almost all the recent increases in federally supported social-science research could be accounted for by increased expenditures by the military agencies.

Of course, we must acknowledge that these patterns are subject to change. Dr. Graham's report was prepared in 1953. Since that time the National Institutes of Mental Health, established by Congress, have supported basic social-science research on a substantial scale. More important, perhaps, is the fact that the National Science Foundation has established a Division of Social Science. The significance of this move lies in the fact that the NSF supports only basic research. As a result of action taken by Congress, the Social Science Division was to have a budget of approximately $7 million in 1962.[26] Although this was only 3.3 per cent of the total NSF budget [27] it represented a marked increase in our national investment in basic social-science research. It is important to notice, as well, that NSF funds are allocated mainly in the form of small grants to individual scholars rather than in large sums for institutional research.

Private foundations, including "giants," such as the Ford Foundation, provide some $15 million annually for social-science research, and from their own resources universities and colleges provide an additional $5 million.[28] Most of the money provided by the foundations, and a substantial part of that furnished by government, is turned over to the universities. As a result, they annually spend about $35 million for social-science research, which is about 16 per cent of the total national expenditure. It is in the university and college that basic research is most likely to be carried on.

[22] Graham, *Federal Utilization.*
[23] *Ibid.*, p. 49.
[24] *Ibid.*, p. 1.
[25] *Ibid.*, p. 38.
[26] *Ibid.*, p. 2.
[27] National Science Foundation, *Federal Funds for Science*, Vol. X, Survey of Science Resources Series, NSF 61–62, p. 23.
[28] Alpert in D. Lerner (ed.), *The Human Meaning of the Social Sciences*, p. 74.

We must then face the fact that only about one eighth of our national expenditure for social research is of the unrestricted, free, or basic variety. The overwhelming bulk of the money is devoted to collecting statistics or to applied research. Anyone who understands the history of science must be distressed to find that the proportion spent on basic research is so low, since it is to it that we must look for those important discoveries and new insights which form the foundation on which progress in applied work depends.

The Bureaucratic Milieu and the Individual Scholar

The sociological profession is growing very rapidly. In 1960 there were about 2,100 living holders of the Ph.D. in sociology.[29] Over half had received their degrees in the preceding 10-year period. Since new Ph.D.'s are graduating at a rate close to 200 per year, in another decade the number will again have doubled. Some critics, for example, C. Wright Mills, would have us believe that this growing corps of highly trained social scientists is being marched, rank on rank, into the insatiable maw of vast research bureaucracies in the government, especially the military establishment, and in advertising offices of business and industry. There these poor young sociologists presumably toil as routinized and bureaucratized intellectual slaves, doing the bidding of masters who have no real interest in social science or its future development. This outcome is a real possibility in the modern world. But the available data fail to support those who claim that the once free intellectual discipline of sociology has been subverted and reduced to a condition of servitude and impotence.

Among the youngest holders of the Ph.D., those under 35, as among the older groups over 55 years of age, approximately three fourths are employed not by large formal research organizations but by colleges and universities. A 1960 survey located only 170 sociologists in the federal government, and of these by far the largest group, numbering 63, was employed in the health, education, and welfare services. There were only 16 in the Department of Defense.[30] Even in the academic world, only 2 per cent of those in regular sociology departments are exclusively in research. Among those not in regular departments, only about 1 in 5 are full-time researchers.[31]

These facts make it difficult to accept C. W. Mills' description of social science as having become bureaucratized, ready "to serve whatever ends its bureaucratic clients have in view." [32] Nor can we quite accept his assertion that: "The idea of a university as a circle of professorial peers, each with apprentices and each practicing a craft, tends to be replaced by the idea of a university as a set of research bureaucracies, each containing an elaborate division of labor, and hence of intellectual technicians." [33]

While acknowledging the growth of large bureaucratic research organizations, we should realize that their activities do not basically change the situation of the individual scholars who still make up the overwhelming majority of the profession. Because some work on "projects" arising out of "programs" of research, rely on professional interviewers and paid research

[29] Sibley, *Education of Sociologists.*

[30] Nahum Z. Medalia and Ward S. Mason, "Position and Prospects of Sociologists in Federal Employment," *American Sociological Review* (1963), XXVIII:282.

[31] Sibley, *op. cit.*

[32] C. Wright Mills, *The Sociological Imagination* (New York: Oxford University Press, 1959), p. 101.

[33] *Ibid.*, p. 103.

assistants, run their data through IBM machines, and juggle their figures on computers, it does not follow that others must do the same.

In any event, the critical fact is that most sociologists are and continue to remain outside the research bureaucracies. The libraries relied on by the classical sociologists who worked as individual craftsmen are as open and free now as they were when Durkheim and Weber wrote their books. It is weak indeed to excuse the failure of one's research to yield results by charging that the other fellow uses bad methods. And many a sociologist who works as an individual craftsman relies heavily on materials assembled by research bureacracies. There is no other way to collect statistics about a large national population or a complicated economic or political system save by developing such an organization. The critical issue is not whether we have research bureaucracies, but what we do with their products. The young sociologist today has the same freedom to do good work, and runs the same risk of doing poor work, as did his predecessor before the era of large-scale research bureaucracies.

Sociology and Social Criticism

Gunnar Myrdal, in a brilliant essay on "The Relation Between Social Theory and Social Policy," [34] argued that the social sciences are important to a democracy because they encourage the open discussion of important issues by appealing to the people's rationality rather than to superstition and narrowness. The sociologist can make this contribution, however, only if his situation affords him reasonable freedom and security.

No doubt some societies and bureaucracies will be more tolerant than others of those who "step out of line." And there are, of course, ways in which the social scientist can work for his ideas within any bureacracy. Nevertheless, most of those employed in public and private agencies which are organized as bureacracies and enforce discipline and loyalty to superiors, will understandably be constrained from playing an independent role either in opening up important issues or in leading people toward their resolution through free public discussion.

Since the overwhelming majority of sociologists are not employed by such special-interest bureaucracies but rather serve as free scholars in the universities and colleges, we might conclude that the situational pressures which might induce them to neglect their obligations to democracy are not great. Ideally the university professor is, in Myrdal's words, "free to pursue the truth without anxiously seeking public acclaim or avoiding public anathema." [35] In practice, as Myrdal, Mills, and others have been quick to point out, the conditions which underlie the professor's independent status may be either very imperfectly assured or lacking altogether.

Three conditions, characteristic of the era following World War II, particularly limit the social scientist's freedom to initiate public discussion of the fundamental issues facing our society.

Professors have become much more deeply involved as advisers to, or grantees of, the government, often moving back and forth between their university town and the seats of power. In 1938 the National Resources Committee complained that "academic men frequently do not know the amount or character of highly interesting scholarly study and research going

[34] Gunnar Myrdal, "The Relation Between Social Theory and Social Policy," *British Journal of Sociology* (1953), XXVII:210–242.

[35] *British Journal of Sociology*, XXIII:218.

on in government [and] governmental agencies do not utilize as fully as they might the intellectual resources of the nation."[36] The same complaint could not be made today with equal justice. As professors develop more intimate contact with government programs, their freedom to criticize those programs becomes limited in various ways. In so far as they share in shaping policy, they are of course not likely to be critics of their own handiwork. Even when they have not participated directly in setting policy, they may be cautious in their criticism so as not to lose their good standing against the day when they *may* be called on. In so far as they rely on government contracts and grants this, of course, introduces an additional restraint.

Not only have individual professors become more intimately involved with government, but so have the universities as such. Some of the leading universities, including those with a very large private endowment, are currently receiving as much as 40 per cent of their total annual budget in the form of grants from and contracts with the federal government. Even in those cases in which a professor is immune to direct pressure, he may be influenced by a desire not to embarrass or harm his university community. In consideration of its interests, he may either temper his remarks or avoid controversial issues altogether. For its part, the university's ability to honor its commitment to the academic freedom of its professors may be pushed beyond the limits of endurance in cases when the university's dependence on public funds is so disproportionately heavy.

By far the most important factors affecting the professor's freedom of expression are the nature of a country's tradition of independence and autonomy for its university, and the climate of opinion which pervades the country at any given time. Many of the European universities enjoy a legally privileged existence which follows custom and law going back to the Middle Ages. Their support by the government is accepted as a traditional obligation which gives public authorities no more right to meddle in the internal affairs of the university than in those of the established church. In addition, the rank and file in Europe often have little awareness of or interest in, and no power to influence, the life of the university and its professors.

It is quite otherwise in the United States. Here the universities, especially the land-grant colleges and the numerous state-supported institutions, were founded to meet the popular demand for education or for practical training in agriculture, the mechanical arts, and the professions. The democratic tradition in America has obliged colleges and universities to adopt relatively open admissions policies. Their financial dependence on state legislatures, and the frequent public review of their budgets by these authorities, make them uncommonly sensitive to public opinion. Often they are open to the influence of every current of public sentiment, however foolish, which sweeps through the community.

The social sciences are particularly vulnerable because in the popular mind—in which category many congressmen and senators are included—the term "sociology" is often understood as being somehow connected with, indeed even the same as, the term "socialism." The problem is rendered all the more acute because sociologists have been outstanding among the few social scientists with the foresight and the courage to undertake systematic study of the emerging societies of Communist countries such as Russia and China. Often their reward for their pains as pioneering students of Communist society was to be mistaken for Communists.

[36] Quoted in Graham, *Federal Utilization*, p. 141.

Sociology and the Free Society

Late in life, Durkheim prepared a contribution on sociology for the volume *La Science Française*, assembled in connection with the San Francisco Exposition of 1915, in which he wrote that sociology could be conceived and develop only in a society which met two conditions:

> First, traditionalism had to have lost its domain. Among a people who consider their institutions everything they ought to be, nothing can incite thought to apply itself to social matters. Second, a veritable faith in the power of reason to dare to undertake the translation of the most complex and unstable of unrealities into definite terms was necessary.[37]

France, said Durkheim, satisfied this double condition. I think we can say that the United States also distinctively fulfilled these conditions. By contrast, the Soviet regime was not long in power in Russia before most of her sociologists were either driven out of the country or purged. Sociology is defined in the Soviet Union as a bourgeois social science, engaged in only by "lackeys" and "wage slaves" of capitalism who use it to counter the "true" Marxist-Leninist social science. Sociology suffered a similar fate in Communist China. Before the Communist takeover, there were more than 1,000 students studying sociology under some 140 teachers in Chinese colleges and universities. The new regime stamped out these activities completely, to replace them by new courses on Marxism. Those sociologists who survive live under a cloud because of their former profession. Dr. Sun Pen-wen, author of what was the leading treatise on sociology before the new regime took over, sent the following chilling response to an American sociologist who wrote requesting a set of his works: "I have come to understand that all my books are only good for burning and hence I have none to send you. I have also learned that I formerly neglected to study the works of Karl Marx which I am now doing many hours a day. Please don't write again." [38]

American society has characteristically subjected itself to a constant process of self-examination and critical reappraisal which has produced a steady stream of proposals for change. Moreover, a surprisingly large number of these has been adopted. As a result, the United States is viewed by most peoples of the world as dynamic and progressive to a degree which they hardly can imagine, and certainly do not expect to realize, for their own countries. This readiness to change has provided an environment conducive to the development of sociology. Americans may justly be proud of the United States' standing as the undisputed world leader in contemporary sociology. This may be considered one of the important confirmations of its outstanding tradition of freedom of thought and inquiry. But that which confirms can also disconfirm. We must acknowledge the recurrent tendencies in American life to subject to political attack those whose scientific investigations are thought too dangerous or whose ideas are too disturbing.

To fulfill the function Myrdal assigns them as searchers for truth and as leaders of the public discussion of basic social issues, sociologists must have security of tenure and some reasonable immunity against political persecution. In England, and probably France, both the tradition and the

[37] Kurt H. Wolff (ed.), *Émile Durkheim* (Columbus: Ohio State University Press, 1960), p. 383.

[38] Albert R. O'Hara, "The Recent Developments of Sociology in China," *American Sociological Review* (1961), XXVI:928.

institutional arrangements guaranteeing independence to the university professor are stronger than in the United States. Where institutional supports are weak, the climate of opinion is all the more important. Dr. Myrdal has said that the "most unfortunate and potentially enormously dangerous effect of the cold war is that even academic discussion tends to be hampered by anxious fore-thoughts and clamped in opportunist stereotypes." [39] The United States has not escaped these effects. The consequences of the atmosphere of suspicion, of thought control, and of punitiveness which prevailed during "the McCarthy era" cannot be realistically assessed by pointing to the small number of professors actually dismissed, nor even by proving that they were really subversives. Much more important is the effect on the free expression of those who were not subversive and who were not dismissed.

Those effects are well-documented in Lazarsfeld and Thielen's study, completed in 1955, of almost 2,500 social-science teachers, including historians, carefully chosen to represent all the colleges and universities in the United States. Of those teaching in larger schools rated as of high quality, 70 per cent reported that they were familiar with at least one "incident" involving an attack on a fellow faculty member for his views or associations. In the smaller and less outstanding schools, 28 per cent of the teachers knew of such incidents.[40] It should not be surprising, therefore, that 40 per cent of college teachers in the social sciences reported that they worried lest some student inadvertently pass on a warped version of what they said,[41] and 22 per cent admitted direct self-censorship of one kind or another.[42] Under such circumstances it is, of course, not only the professor who suffers but equally the students and the community, which are denied the chance to hear a frank expression of the views of men especially well-qualified to analyze our society and its problems.

Sociology can thrive only under freedom. Indeed, the extent to which sociologists may pursue their interests, fully publish their results, and freely state their conclusions is one important index of the degree to which a nation qualifies as a free and open society. A nation cannot have quality in sociology by fiat. It can, if it chooses, write a kind of "contract" for that kind of sociology which guarantees, in advance, to produce results which affirm the established order and confirm received doctrine. It may then get what it orders, as it does in the Soviet Union, but it will not get good sociology. Only a nation which provides the conditions for free inquiry may with reason hope for the development of social-science knowledge which permits ever deeper understanding of man in society.

[39] *British Journal of Sociology*, XXIII:222.

[40] Paul Lazarsfeld and Wagner Thielens, Jr., *The Academic Mind* (Glencoe, Ill.: The Free Press, 1958), p. 164.

[41] *Ibid.*, p. 76.

[42] *Ibid.*, p. 78.

selected references

The following material only suggests the extent of the literature in the field available to anyone who wishes to read background material in the classics of sociology, basic concepts and/or statements of the contemporary field.

Additional textbooks, useful for an over-all glance and prominent in the discipline are: Leonard Broom and Philip Selznick, *Sociology: A Text with Adapted Readings* (Evanston: Row, Peterson, 1955); Arnold Green, *Sociology—An Analysis of the Life of Modern Society,* 3rd ed. (New York: McGraw-Hill, 1956); and William F. Ogburn and Meyer F. Nimkoff, *Sociology,* 3rd ed. (Boston: Houghton Mifflin, 1958).

General discussion and presentation of current trends in the field and profession can be found in: S. Martin Lipset and Neil Smelser (eds.), *Sociology: The Progress of a Decade* (Englewood Cliffs, N. J.: Prentice-Hall, 1961); Robert K. Merton, Leonard Broom, and Leonard S. Cottrell, Jr., *Sociology Today: Problems and Prospects* (New York: Basic Books, 1959); Edward Shils, "The Calling of Sociology," Epilogue to Talcott Parsons, *et al.* (eds.), *Theories of Society,* two volumes (Glencoe, Ill.: The Free Press, 1961); and Hans L. Zetterberg, *Sociology in the United States: A Trend Report* (Paris: UNESCO, 1956).

Professional journals that offer statements concerning the state of the field and current empirical and theoretical studies are: *American Journal of Sociology, American Sociological Review, British Journal of Sociology, Daedalus,* and *Human Organization.* The *Journal of Conflict Resolution, Journal of Intergroup Relations, Journal of Social Issues, Social Forces, Social Problems,* and *Sociometry* are also useful.

Contemporary works that present basic concepts and approaches to analyses of social systems and illustrate the use of sociological tools are (to name a few): Kingsley Davis, *Human Society* (New York: Macmillan, 1949); George C. Homans, *The Human Group* (New York: Harcourt, Brace & World, 1950); Marion Levy, *The Structure of Society* (Princeton: Princeton University Press, 1948); Robert M. MacIver, *Society: Its Structure and Changes* (New York: Long and Smith, 1931); Robert K. Merton, *Social Theory and Social Structure,* rev. ed. (Glencoe, Ill.: The Free Press, 1956); Talcott Parsons, *Essays in Sociological Theory: Pure and Applied* (Glencoe, Ill.: The Free Press, 1949); and Robin Williams, *American Society* (New York: Knopf, 1951).

For three examples of a discussion of philosophy of science and social science see: Morris Cohen, *Reason and Nature: An Essay on the Meaning of Scientific Method* (New York: Harcourt, Brace & World, 1931); Morris Cohen and Ernest Nagel, *An Introduction to Logic and the Scientific Method* (New York: Harcourt, Brace & World, 1936); and Ernest Nagel, *Structure of Science* (New York: Harcourt, Brace & World, 1961).

For illustrations of the use of mathematical models and stochastic processes see: James S. Coleman, *Mathematical Sociology* (Englewood Cliffs, N. J.: Prentice-Hall, 1964); Anatol Rapaport, *Fights, Games and Debates* (Ann Arbor: University of Michigan Press, 1960); Herbert A. Simon, *Models of Man: Social and Rational* (New York: Wiley, 1957); John Von Neumann and Oskar Morgenstern, *Theory of Games and Economic Behavior,* 2nd ed. (Princeton: Princeton University Press, 1947); and Harrison C. White, *Anatomy of Kinship* (Englewood Cliffs, N. J.: Prentice-Hall, 1963).

For the works of some of the classical figures in sociology refer to the footnotes and text.

index